Louise Fox lives with her partner and three children. This is her first book.

Mummy, Make It Stop

Louise Fox

headline
review

First published in 2009
by HEADLINE REVIEW
An imprint of HEADLINE PUBLISHING GROUP

1

Cataloguing in Publication Data is available from the British Library

978 0 7553 1850 6

Typeset in Dante by Palimpsest Book Production Limited
Grangemouth, Stirlingshire

Printed and bound in Great Britain by
Clays Ltd, St Ives plc

Headline's policy is to use papers that are natural, renewable and recyclable products and
made from wood grown in sustainable forests. The logging and manufacturing processes
are expected to conform to the environmental regulations of the country of origin.

HEADLINE PUBLISHING GROUP
An Hachette UK Company
338 Euston Road
London NW1 3BH

www.headline.co.uk
www.hachette.co.uk

For my guardian angel and
my three beautiful girls

Chapter One

'Louise . . . upstairs.'

The voice summoning me was cold and harsh. I tried to swallow, but my mouth was too dry.

I looked at my brother and sister, who were sitting on either side of me on the sofa. The three of us had been staring at the television, but we weren't really watching it; we were too scared. They nodded at me to go.

I wanted to run away. Run and run. Anywhere, rather than face what was coming. But there was no escape, and I knew I had better not be too slow. So I got up and walked out of the living room and across the hall.

As I reached the bottom of the stairs, I could see his shadow on the wall. The shadow of my stepdad, George. He was on the landing at the top, waiting for me. I tried to switch off my fear and make myself numb. It was the only way to bear it.

George was a big man, six feet tall, wiry and strong, with thick, wavy brown hair that he tried to control with dollops of hair cream, and a pasty face. As I got to the top of the stairs, his large frame towered over me. He was standing in his usual place, next to the small window on the landing. The light coming through the net curtains made me squint as I looked up at him. I arched my neck to see his face, because I didn't want to look at his body. He was completely naked.

He looked down at me.

'OK, let's do the dusting,' he ordered.

Without a word I dropped to my knees, and he did the same, before pushing his erect penis into my face and then forcing it into my mouth.

He grabbed hold of my hair and forced himself down my throat, pulling my head back so that I had to look into his cold blue eyes. As he thrust into me my head was thrown from side to side and my eyes watered, as I tried not to choke. I prayed that it would be over soon, and that he wouldn't make me swallow the nasty, sticky stuff that came out of his penis.

I retched and tried to pull away, but he shouted at me to keep it in my mouth and swallow, promising me an ice cream. I did as he said; not for the ice cream, because there never was one, but because I was too scared to do anything else. His body juddered and his grip on my hair loosened, but he ordered me to keep 'dusting' with my hand until he was finished.

Finally, he let out a huge breath of air and it was over. 'Go back downstairs,' he ordered, before walking off towards the bathroom.

As I made my way downstairs I still had the foul taste in my mouth and I felt as if the messy stuff was stuck at the back of my throat. Sometimes George let me get a drink from the bathroom tap afterwards, but this time he had refused.

I could still smell him as I walked back into the living room and sat back down in my place. This time I didn't look at my brother and sister. I simply stared at the television again, hoping that something on the screen would take my mind away for a short time, and help me forget what had just gone on. But nothing could. Nothing took away the empty, scared, sick feeling inside.

I was five years old, and George had been calling me up the stairs like this since I was three. My sister, Tanya, who was eight, and my brother, Jamie, who was seven, had to 'do the dusting' too, although I seemed to be his favourite. Our older brother, Paul, was twelve and he'd been sent out on an errand. George didn't make Paul go upstairs with him – I suppose because he was older – but he treated him like dirt.

We should all have been in school, but on this day, like so many others, George had refused to let us go. While Mum was out at work, stacking shelves in a local supermarket, George kept us at home and made us sit in front of the TV – though we were never allowed to choose what to watch – while he called one of us, or sometimes all of us, one by one, up the stairs.

Although George was not my dad, I couldn't remember the

time before we lived with him. When my real dad left Mum with four small children, we had all moved into George's house within weeks.

He lived on a notorious estate in a rough part of Manchester, where endless streets of ugly, grey council houses sat back to back, with only a few balding patches of grass here and there to break the monotony. Ours was a three-bedroom semi. The boys shared the smallest room, George and Mum had the biggest and Tanya and I had the middle one. All the houses looked the same from the outside, but ours was one of the better ones on the estate on the inside. Mum and George insisted on keeping things clean and tidy, with everything in its place.

The furnishings were very basic. The room Tanya and I shared had cream walls and a cord carpet and a big, old-fashioned, dark-wood wardrobe. We slept on old metal-framed bunk-beds, though we had them as singles, not bunks. My hair often used to catch in the metal frame and I'd have to yank it free. We weren't allowed to put any pictures on the walls, and we had very few toys – just a teddy or two and a couple of dolls.

George had lived in the house with his wife and two children, and when his marriage split up, they left and he stayed on. He and Mum met in the shop where she worked, when he did his shopping there, and when Mum found herself on her own too, I suppose they kept one another company, and that grew into something more. But even though he made us call him 'Dad', they never actually married.

George, unlike my real dad, was not a drinker at all – he never went to the pub. He would keep himself to himself at all times, and everyone around us knew not to cross him. His voice had a quiet, menacing tone that no-one dared to question, including Mum.

George was quite a bit older than Mum. But although he was only in his mid-forties, he didn't have a job. I'm not sure what they lived on, because Mum's wages and child benefit can't have been much. We certainly didn't have much money – our clothes were always worn and tatty, and we had to use cut-up newspaper instead of toilet paper.

Although he very seldom left the house, George insisted on dressing smartly every day. He was obsessive about ironing his clothes – his trousers always had to be pressed with a crease, and his shirts perfect. He behaved as though he was going to work and had to be perfectly turned out, even though he wasn't going anywhere.

He ran the house using rigid rules, and anyone who disobeyed him was thrashed. None of us was allowed to speak unless we were spoken to. We were taught what to say and when to say it. We never dared disagree with or question anything. We did as we were told, because we knew what would happen if we didn't.

George spent most of his time sitting in his favourite chair in front of the TV, drinking endless cups of strong, sweet tea from his favourite mug, which no-one else was allowed to touch. If he kept us home from school, we had to sit in front of the TV with him, all of us lined up on the sofa. We were never allowed to watch kids' programmes, so we were bored and restless, but we didn't dare show it.

A short while after Mum left for work, George would get up and go upstairs, and we knew it was time. One of us would be called up to do the dusting. We waited, barely able to breathe, to hear who it would be.

Every now and then, when Mum was out, he'd decide to show us some films, to 'educate' us. They were porn films of the worst kind. He would sit us in front of one of them and he'd sit beside us as we watched. I didn't really understand what was going on with all these writhing, jerking bodies. I felt bored and wished we could watch something else, but George insisted we keep our eyes fixed on the telly.

I always thought Mum knew about George and the dusting. He generally did it when she was at work, or on the two evenings a week when she went out to bingo. But sometimes he did it while she was in the house, downstairs. She would have had to be blind and deaf not to know that something was going on. At the time I just thought all this was normal – George making us do the dusting, Mum knowing about it – because George told us it was what all families did. He would tell us that this was what people who loved each other did. Mum did the dusting for him, and when she was at work it was our turn. Whenever I called for one of my friends and no-one answered the door, I imagined that they were upstairs with their dad, doing the dusting.

George was clever. I'm sure he called it 'the dusting' so that if we ever talked about it, people would think we meant housework. But we never did talk about it. Even though we thought it was what everyone did, we somehow knew George wouldn't want us to mention it.

After we had spent a long, miserable morning sitting in front of the TV and being called upstairs by George, Mum would come home. At least then there was no more dusting, but in other respects things weren't much better. Mum was just as hard on us as George was. She either ignored us or shouted at us. Neither of them ever showed any of us the tiniest bit of affection. There were no cuddles, smiles or questions about our day. Mum knew we hadn't been to school, but she didn't say a thing. George's word was law.

Mum would make tea at four thirty each day. George, despite being at home all day, did no housework or cooking at all. Mum would come out of the kitchen with her plate of food and one for George, and they would settle in their chairs in front of the TV. Then she'd nod towards the kitchen and tell us to get ours. We'd take our plates and eat on our knees on the sofa. We had a drop-leaf dining table that stood in the living room, but we only ever ate off it on the rare occasions when George's two children came to visit, or at Christmas.

We ate what we were given, whether we were hungry or not. There was trouble if anything was left on our plates. None of us would have dared to say we didn't like the food, although Mum was no cook, so it was often pretty tasteless. Mostly we had sausages or egg, with chips and beans, though at weekends we had liver, which we kids all hated. Sometimes it was served with sprouts, which made Tanya gag. Afterwards, we kids washed and dried the dishes and did our chores – bringing in the washing or tidying our rooms. We were sent to bed at 6.30, even on long, light summer evenings, while Mum and George stayed in front of the telly.

Once a week it was bath night. The bath was run twice, first for me and Tanya and then for Paul and Jamie. I hated bath night. I was always at the plug end, and although Mum was in the house, it was always George who bathed us. He seemed to take pleasure in being cruel – especially to me. For some reason, he always had it in for me more than Tanya. He would wash my hair and hold my head under the water, or put loads of shampoo in my eyes to make me cry. When he held me under the water, my nose would sting and I'd start to struggle, getting more and more frightened, until he let me go, just as my lungs were about to burst. I soon came to dread bath night, and tried to get out of it, but there was no escape.

Goodness knows what kept Mum and George together.

They didn't row – I think Mum knew better than to cross George – but there was never any laughter or warmth between them. I think Mum liked being with George because everyone else was scared of him. Even though she was scared of him herself, being with a big, intimidating man like him gave her a sense of power. If people were scared of George, then they were scared of her too, and she liked that.

Mum never had any friends; she didn't seem to know how to be friendly. She was always thinking that people were out to get her. According to her, all the neighbours were the enemy, and wanted to hurt us. Secretly, I didn't think they seemed like the enemy at all. Some of them smiled at me in a friendly way, and I wished that we could be friends with them. But even if she managed to start a friendship, Mum soon fell out with them. She'd borrow money and not pay it back, or badmouth the person, or accuse them of something.

That's one thing Mum and George shared – a hatred of the neighbours. Not that the two of them talked to one another much. Mostly they sat in front of the TV in silence. They may not have talked much, but they still had a sex life. They would go upstairs together sometimes and we could all hear them at it, grunting away, while we sat downstairs, too scared to move, even when they weren't in the room.

It certainly wasn't Mum's looks that George went for; she looked really rough.

She was only thirty-one but she looked a lot older. She was

short and very overweight – she must have been a size eighteen or twenty – with peroxide-blonde hair that she dyed herself, and her arms were covered with ugly scars from where she had cut herself. I hated to see them – I couldn't imagine why she had hurt herself so badly – but she said it had been when she was younger and didn't know what she was doing.

Mum was the youngest of four sisters. She was born on the estate and her parents still lived nearby, but her mother, who we called Nanna, was a long way from being a cuddly granny. Slight, with small features, she was grumpy and irritable. We never saw her smile, and she constantly had a cigarette in her mouth and a mug of tea in her hand and was often agitated. She worked in a clothing factory and spent her evenings at bingo. She was certainly never happy to see us. We never got presents or cards from her, and though most of the time she ignored us, she could lash out. Once she turned the rings on her fingers around before slapping Tanya, so that the stones in the rings cut her face.

Our grandfather was even worse. He spent his time fixing old cars outside their house, and Mum told us he used to beat her when she was a child. I thought he looked scary, but I never found out if he really was, because he took even less notice of us than Nanna did.

Most of the time, when she wasn't at work, Mum lay around in front of the TV, eating sweets. She would buy herself big chocolate bars and I'd watch her eating them, longing for a little bit but not daring to ask. She'd look at me, grin, and then stick the whole lot in her mouth. She'd lie on the floor, with her feet on the sofa, and we'd have to rub cream into them, or tickle them, for hours at a time. Sometimes she'd make us draw with a pen on her back, because she liked the feeling, and then afterwards we had to wash it all off.

The atmosphere in our house was always tense and fearful. We felt we were walking on eggshells all the time. We crept around, trying as hard as we could not to upset Mum or George. No-one relaxed, or laughed, or chatted, or even spoke in a normal voice. George kept us all silent and permanently on edge with a chilling look that we knew meant 'Cross me, and you know what you'll get.'

We knew all too well. If we did anything wrong, like talking out of place, or dropping something, or not being quick enough to do a chore, or eating something we weren't allowed, then George or Mum would order us upstairs for a beating.

Mum didn't beat us herself – apart from the odd whack on the back of the head, or slap on the back of the legs. But she threatened us all the time. She used to put her clenched fist and her angry face right up against yours and say things like 'Carry on 'n' I'll knock ya block off' or 'I'll knock your fuckin' head clean off ya shoulders' or 'I'll hit you so hard you won't be able to sit for a week.' But she let George do the thrashing. She would sit downstairs in front of the telly, listening to whoever was being hit screaming in agony, and she wouldn't react at all, she just carried on as normal.

As for George, he really seemed to enjoy it. It was impossible not to cry as you went up the stairs, knowing what was coming. We all tried to swallow back the tears, because if George saw you crying, he would beat you even more. He would be up there waiting, taking off his belt and flexing it so that it made snapping sounds, an evil glint in his eye.

For some reason he always punished us in Jamie and Paul's little room. It stank in there, because Jamie wet the bed, and more often than not the sheets didn't get changed. Jamie got beaten for wetting the bed, but it didn't make any difference, he couldn't help it. He stank all the time, and in the bedroom the rancid, sour smell of stale urine was so bad that most of the time the door was kept shut.

George would make you pull down your pants, and then kneel down and lean over the bottom bunk-bed. Then he'd hit you with the belt, sometimes using the buckle end, until your tender skin was a mass of welts and cuts.

We all dreaded the beatings, and we all got beaten, no matter how hard we tried to be good. Tanya once got beaten for breaking a vase when she hadn't been near it. But it was Paul who suffered most. He was our half-brother – Mum had him when she was nineteen, before she met our dad – and both she and George seemed to have it in for him even more than for the rest of us. Nothing he ever did was right, and he was beaten more often and more viciously.

Virtually the only time George ever left the house was once a week, on Saturdays, when we all went to his mum's house for lunch. We called her Nanna Gladice. She was very small and old and was partially blind and hard of hearing, so we always had to talk loudly to her. She had a cup which beeped, so that she could find it, and I was fascinated by it.

His brother, Trevor, would be there too. I liked these outings, because George's mum and brother were both really nice. His mum would fuss over us, making beans on toast for lunch and giving each of us 50p.

On the way home from Nanna Gladice's we would go to Morrisons and do the shopping, which we would all help to carry home. Sometimes we kids got a booty bag each – a bag with sweets and little toys in it. I loved those booty bags and used to look forward to them all week. When we got home I would go up to my room to open mine, looking excitedly to see what I'd got. Sometimes there was a little colouring book and crayons, sometimes a little plastic toy. I would sit on my bed playing with them for hours.

Once a month or so, George's children, Chelsea and Lauren came over. They lived ten minutes away, so we'd walk over and collect them on our way to visit Nanna Gladice. We waited at their house while they got ready, and I was fascinated by what a mess it was. Their mum, Sue, had pots and pans all over the kitchen and clutter absolutely everywhere. They had a massive fish tank and a big, scary dog that bounded all over the place. It was so different from our house that I wondered how George and Sue had ever managed to be married.

Chelsea was the same age as Jamie – and, just like him, she was plump – although she was actually friendlier with Paul. Lauren was the same age as Tanya. They seemed all right, but we never really got to know them, because they were only with us for three or four hours and for most of that time George would be organising what everyone was doing. He would make a big effort to be pleasant and charming in front of them and we'd all have to play a game together, like Monopoly. After that we'd have tea at the table, and George would help to make it, keen to make a good impression on his kids.

They never stayed the night, and years later I discovered that this was because George had been caught masturbating in front of them. They were protected from him – yet he had been allowed to move in with us and we had no protection from him at all.

After Chelsea and Lauren went, the games would be put away, the table pushed back into place, the smile would vanish from George's face and he would go back to snapping and snarling at us. This dramatic change in him, the minute his kids were out of the door, made it crystal clear just how little George thought of us.

These Saturday routines – lunch and shopping, or games and tea on the days George's kids came over – were the only little bit of normality we had as a family. Afterwards it was back to silence and fear and beatings.

I was only five, but I felt that my life was like being on a train in a dark tunnel that wasn't going to come to an end, so there would never be light again. I used to cope by switching off and going into my own world, a world where no-one hurt me, where I got hugs and kindness and where I could feel happy and loved and wanted.

Chapter Two

The best days for me were the ones when I was allowed to go to school. Tanya could take or leave school, Paul hated it and Jamie wasn't too keen, but I loved it – it always smelled nice and I felt happy there, even though I never really fitted in or made any real friends.

It wasn't just that I preferred sitting in the classroom to being at home, at George's mercy. There was something about school that drew me like a magnet; I loved the idea of learning.

Catton Primary School was a short journey away from our house – go up a couple of narrow lanes between the houses and along two streets and you were there. I walked the ten-minute journey with Tanya and Jamie, though he would often bunk off and go to his friends' houses. Paul was already at the secondary school, so he went a different route.

Our day would always start with a visit to the shop round the corner from our house. We would wait for a couple of other people to go in and follow them. Jamie would keep a lookout and then, while the shopkeeper was busy with the other customers, Tanya and I would stuff any goodies we could reach into our coats and up our sleeves. I wasn't very good at it in the beginning, and I'd come out with almost nothing. But I soon caught on and we'd come out of the shop with pockets full of sweets and crisps and biscuits and keep them there all the way to school, when we'd hide them in our coats while we went into class.

The school was huge; most of the kids from the three surroundings estates went there. And the classes were big too. We had a nice young teacher who was very kind. But I hid at the back of the class. I felt shy and afraid of being asked to do anything in case I messed it up. I used to sit with my head down and go bright red if anyone spoke to me. Once the teacher asked me to read out loud and I stood looking at the book, blushing and stuttering as I tried to get the words out. She didn't ask me again after that.

Lessons were often confusing for me, because I missed so much school. Things often made no sense to me, and I was forever trying to catch up. But rather than helping me, the teacher would often tell me not to worry about trying to join in, preferring me to sit there and draw or just watch everyone else. It was a shame, because I wanted to learn. I didn't want to be different from everyone else.

I thought I was thick. It was many years before I realised that I was actually pretty bright, and could have done well if I'd had the chance. Despite missing so much school, I had learned to read by the time I was five. And I liked maths and wasn't bad at sums.

I was generally either ignored or bullied by the other kids. Being away half the time, I never had a chance to really fit in. And they could see that I was different. A lot of us were poor, but I was the only one in grubby, stained clothes and worn-out shoes.

There were two playgrounds – one for the older kids and another for the younger ones. Tanya was in the older half, so I didn't get to see her at breaktimes very often. Mostly I would sit on a wall in the corner of the infants' playground, watching all the other children playing – chasing each other, kicking balls around and skipping. No-one asked me to play, and mostly I didn't mind – I was content just watching. I was used to being on my own, keeping quiet and not saying much – that was how we had to live our lives at home, so I didn't expect it to be different at school and I didn't expect anyone to ask me to play, or want to be my friend. I longed to have friends and to be popular like Naomi Watson – who was so good at running that she won medals for it – or as pretty as Amber Smith. But I was a small, plump kid and I hardly ever spoke, because I didn't know what to say to people. So they tended to ignore me, or if they did decide to talk to me, it was to call me names and pick on me.

I was jealous of all the girls around me. They looked so nice in their pretty ankle socks, shiny black patent shoes and lovely dresses. I wore shoes with holes in them, dirty over-the-knee socks that I rolled down to make them look like ankle socks, and a threadbare dress that had seen better days. My blonde hair was never brushed and George had cut it into a bob with a straight fringe two inches too short, making it look as if my forehead was too big. Yet another excuse for everyone to have a good laugh at me.

Sometimes I was jealous of Tanya too. She was slim and dark-haired and pretty, and although she had to wear the same tatty old clothes as me, she was a lot more confident and somehow managed to make plenty of friends. I wished I could be like her, but I just didn't know how. Tanya never seemed lost for words, she didn't go bright red if someone spoke to her, and she wasn't afraid to join in the other kids' games.

I loved Tanya. She was the person I was closest to in the world. Although I got jealous of her, and sometimes we fought and fell out, most of the time we were pals. We shared a room, and sometimes even a bed. If I was feeling sad or scared, Tanya would let me climb in beside her. I always felt a bit stronger if she was close by.

Perversely, George would make us go to school if we were ill. On one occasion I had caught impetigo and Mum had covered my mouth and chin completely in Gentian Violet, a bright purple ointment that was supposed to get rid of it. That day I was made to go to school. I cried and cried, saying I couldn't go, but George took great delight in saying that I wasn't staying at home with him looking like that. I hid for most of the time in the cloakrooms as the rest of the kids went about their normal day. But I couldn't avoid everyone – some of them saw me and laughed their heads off at the way I looked, and I wished I could just melt through the floor and disappear.

The only time I had a taste of what it was like to be popular was when I pulled out the goodies I had stolen from the shop. I would bring them into the playground and then beam with delight as more and more kids crowded round to see what I had brought in that day. I loved the attention and milked every minute of it, trying to buy as many friends as I could as I handed out my biscuits and crisps. But no sooner had the last biscuit gone than so had all the kids and I would be left standing on my own. I'd go back to my usual spot on the wall in the corner of the schoolyard and watch everyone else play and laugh and have fun.

Then, one day, something amazing happened. I had been handing out Bourbon biscuits to everyone when I noticed that for the first time Amber Smith was in the group of people reaching out to me. I had always admired Amber – she always looked so clean and pretty and happy. She had loads of friends, seemed to know everyone and everyone knew and liked her.

My packet was almost empty, so I quickly grabbed one and handed it to Amber, smiling and hoping that she would smile back and stand near me for a minute longer. For a moment I felt a glow of happiness – one of the most popular girls in our year was standing with me.

As my last Bourbon was snatched away, the crowds disappeared, leaving me alone on my wall. Then Amber walked past me and handed me an envelope, saying, 'You can come over earlier if you want to play at my house.' I couldn't believe it. What did she mean?

I stood there staring at the envelope. My name was written clearly on the front in black pen. The envelope was pink, with fairies on the front and little clouds on the back. It looked so pretty I didn't want to rip it so I spent the rest of the morning break carefully pulling it open, a tiny bit at a time. When at last I opened the folded piece of paper inside I could hardly believe it. It was an invitation to Amber's birthday party the following week.

That afternoon I ran home feeling so excited. As soon as I got in, I told Mum about the invitation. She looked irritated and snapped, 'Don't expect to take a present for her. And you'll have to get someone to take you there, because I'm not.' My whole body deflated. I should have known that Mum wouldn't care. But at least she had said I could go. For the next few days I hugged that thought to me.

On the day of the party, a Saturday, I woke up earlier than normal in anticipation, my head spinning with excitement. I tried to imagine the party; I had never been to anyone's house before, and I had certainly never been to a party. I didn't know what to expect, but I was sure it would be lovely.

To my relief, Mum had got a card for me to give to Amber. At least I wouldn't have to turn up with nothing. I didn't have anything nice to wear – just an old skirt with the same old long socks I had to wear for school and my school shoes with holes in them. But even that didn't dampen my spirits. By noon I was so excited I barely knew what to do with myself. I told Mum that Amber had said I could go earlier and play at her house before the party started, hoping that I could go really early. But Mum said no, and that I wouldn't be going anywhere until the party started.

I was beside myself with disappointment. I went to my room and sat on the bed. Why couldn't I go? I was desperate to go, no-one had ever wanted me to come and play before. Then I thought of a plan. What if I went early, and Mum didn't know? I could just pretend I was playing outside, and then sneak off. I didn't know where to go, but that was OK, because she had told me to get someone to take me.

As the time approached, I told Mum I was going to play out for while and she said OK. Then I went and found Paul, who was hanging about outside, and told him that Mum had said that he had to walk me to the party, as it was across the park. He agreed and we set off.

As we made our way across the park, my heart was

jumping. I had never felt so excited and I didn't even think about what would happen if Mum found out I had defied her. I thought my plan was foolproof.

Paul dropped me off at the bottom of Amber's street and I walked along, looking at the house numbers, until I saw hers. The street was much smarter than any I had seen before, and as I went up towards the front door my excitement gave way to nerves. The garden looked as though someone had spent a lot of time caring for the plants and making sure everything seemed just perfect. I stopped for a moment and gazed at it, thinking how pretty the flowers were.

As I approached, I saw Amber at the front window. I waved, and she came rushing to open the door for me. She looked beautiful in a gorgeous party dress with little white ankle socks and patent shoes. Her blonde hair was shiny and I wanted to touch it because it looked so nice and soft. She was beaming from ear to ear and yelled at me to come on inside.

The house was just as nice on the inside as it was on the outside. It felt warm and welcoming and as I stood in the hall I could see through the open doors that the rooms were painted in lovely colours and were full of beautiful things. On the hall wall was a picture of Amber and her family all sitting together, with her mum and dad's arms around her and her brother. They all looked so happy and cared for.

Just then Amber's mum appeared in the hallway.

'Hi, you must be Louise,' she said, smiling.

Nervously, I nodded and tried to smile back. Her voice was so calm and gentle and she was smiling at me, even though she didn't know me. Why would she be like that? Mum and George were never like that – they always seemed agitated by us kids and we wouldn't have dared ask any other child back to our house.

Amber's mum was so kind that I soon began to relax. Just then, Katie, another girl from school, turned up and Amber's mum suggested we go upstairs to play until the rest of the children arrived.

Amber's room was wonderful. She had a bunk-bed and desk all in one, with the bed bit at the top. My eyes were racing around the room, spotting Barbie dolls, prams, games and loads of stuff I had always dreamed of having. I had asked every year for the last three years for a Barbie doll for my birthday or for Christmas, but it never came. I could hardly believe that Amber had several.

She had fairies all over her wallpaper and a border in pink and purple going all round her room. I thought it looked just like a little girl's room should. I felt so happy. Amber and her mum seemed to like me and want to be with me and I wished I could stay with them forever.

Katie and I sat on the floor and Amber showed us the presents she'd got from her family. I couldn't help but feel jealous at the array of lovely things she had. I had never known anything like that. In our house birthdays were a non-event. We were lucky to get a small present. Usually we just got a fiver, but somehow the money was always 'borrowed' back by Mum, so I never got to spend it.

When the other children arrived we went downstairs. The rooms were decorated with birthday banners and ribbons, balloons were tied up everywhere and there must have been about twelve or thirteen birthday cards on the window sill – and that was before any of Amber's school friends' cards had been added. The kitchen table had a princess tablecloth with 'happy birthday' written across it, and paper plates lay on place-mats ready for the piles of gorgeous-looking party food laid out on the table. There were several adults there and they were smiling and talking to each other calmly – no-one was shouting or fighting or pointing aggressively, like our Mum did.

Amber's mum kept coming up to her and touching her shoulders gently and hugging her, or kissing her forehead. I watched her, fascinated and filled with longing, wishing that she would hug and kiss me too. I had never been treated that way by anyone, Mum never hugged or kissed me, not even on my birthday or at Christmas, though I often wished she would. Sometimes when I was feeling really down I would sit next to her and start to try to nudge myself under her arm and onto her knee, hoping she would give me a hug or a cuddle, but she would just push me away and tell me to sit somewhere else. I never felt that she really liked me.

The party was just getting going, and we were about to play a game, when Amber's dad came into the room. Smiling kindly, he took me quietly to one side and told me my brother was downstairs and that I had to go home straightaway.

I stared at him, horrified. Surely I wasn't going to have to leave this lovely place, the wonderful party I had looked forward to so much and that had barely got started? Surely Mum wouldn't be so unkind?

I wanted it to be some kind of mistake. I looked towards Amber, hoping she would plead with me to stay, but she was lost in her new toys and surrounded by friends.

I walked slowly downstairs behind Amber's dad, trying to put off the moment when I would have to leave this magical place and go back to face what I knew was coming.

Paul was standing in the doorway. He looked up and said, 'Mum wants you home, NOW.' Reluctantly, I followed him out of the door. I turned back and saw Amber's dad smiling at me from the doorway. He waved before he closed the door.

All my excitement and happiness evaporated as I followed Paul back across the park in silence. I tried not to think about what was waiting for me back at home, but my eyes started to fill with tears as I begged Paul to tell me what Mum had said to him. He just kept quiet the whole way, which only confirmed that I was in serious trouble.

Paul didn't come in with me. He left me at the door and turned to go. He looked over his shoulder at me as he rounded the corner. I could see in his eyes that he felt for me. None of us ever liked seeing one of the others punished. We had all been there too often.

I opened the front door as quietly as I could, and tiptoed into the house, hoping that by some miracle everything had been forgotten and I wouldn't be punished. I could see Mum sitting in her chair, eyes fixed on the television screen. She turned and saw me, and got up, her face thunderous.

'How dare you defy me? This will be the last time you disobey me, you little cow.' Her voice didn't sound like it normally did when we were in trouble; it was calmer. George was standing just behind her, his face expressionless, staring at me.

'Upstairs,' he barked.

He marched past me and straight upstairs as I looked pleadingly at Mum, wishing she would help me. She looked at me coldly and nodded towards the stairs. 'Go on,' she said. Then she walked back to her chair and sat down.

Tears began to roll down my cheeks and I couldn't move my feet. Fifteen minutes earlier I had never felt so happy. Now I was petrified, and I knew there was nothing I could do to avoid what was coming.

Slowly, I made my way upstairs. George was waiting in the doorway to the boys' room. As I reached the landing, he grabbed hold of my arm and dragged me to the bottom bunkbed. He pushed me face down on the bed, pulling my skirt up and ripping my knickers down. I could hear him flexing his belt as he stood there above me.

'I'll make sure you can't go anywhere for a week,' he snarled.

Four powerful lashes later, he was gone, leaving me crying on the floor, my bottom raw and bleeding and my knickers still round my ankles. I lay there for a long time, in too much pain and shock to even cry.

Eventually, I managed to drag myself into my room, where I crawled onto my bed. I lay there thinking about the party and how much fun everyone would be having. I imagined the games they would all be playing, and Amber's mum, with her kind face, smiling, and the delicious food I never got to taste. I cuddled my teddy bear and cried into his soft fur.

On Monday morning, back at school, I was treated just as I had always been. No-one spoke to me, and I retreated silently to the wall in the playground. I watched Amber and her friends playing, but she didn't even look at me. Was she angry that I had left? Or had she simply forgotten all about me? I guessed that was it. It was as though I had never been to her party, or had that precious glimpse into her life.

But I never forgot a single moment of it. After that day, I used to lie in bed, thinking of Amber's lovely home, and pretty room, and kind parents. Now I knew that those things existed, even if I couldn't have them. And I dreamed that one day I might live in a world like Amber Smith's.

Chapter Three

Soon after my sixth birthday, which was a complete non-event in our house, my class teacher announced that she wanted fifteen children to take part in a May Day dance performed for the parents.

The hairs on my arms stood on end as she explained that the lucky fifteen would be dancing around a maypole. As soon as she asked for volunteers, my arm shot up as high as I could hold it. While most of the time I tried hard not to be noticed or picked for anything, dancing was different. I loved dancing more than anything. Tanya and I sometimes practised little dance routines in our room, but that was all I'd ever done. Now there was a chance to do some proper dancing at school, and my shyness fell away in my eagerness to be included.

I looked around the room. Almost everyone had their hands up as well. What chance did I have? I was sure I wouldn't be picked because I had been chosen for a school performance before and I'd had to drop out, after I missed too many rehearsals what with George keeping us at home all the time. I'd also been chosen as an angel in the nativity play the previous Christmas, and I was even given a few lines to say. But again I missed so many rehearsals that they had to drop the lines and just let me appear in the background.

The teacher began calling the names of the girls and boys she wanted. She called so many out that I thought that must be it. But then she looked at me, smiled and called out 'Louise'. I was so happy I thought I would burst.

We had two weeks before the performance and would be having rehearsals over five lunch breaks. Each of us was given a letter to take home, explaining that we had been selected for this event, what we would need to wear and when the final performance was to be. The parents of the dancers were to be given front-row seats.

My heart was jumping for the rest of the day, and by the time the bell went for home time my face had began to ache from smiling. I was determined that I would be at school for the rehearsals and the performance. This time I would make it.

I ran all the way home with the letter grasped tightly in my hand. Mum wouldn't be back for a couple of hours, so I decided to keep quiet till she arrived, rather than give it to George. He would throw it straight into the bin and tell me I could forget it. At least with Mum I would have a chance of making it.

As soon as she came in I ran up to her with the letter. She didn't look in a good mood at all.

'What now?' she scowled. I hesitated, and then decided to

tell her all about it, hoping she would be happy when she heard.

'I've been picked for the May Day dance,' I explained excitedly. Her expression didn't change. She took the letter and walked off into the living room, where George and Jamie were watching television.

I followed her. 'I need you to sign it for me to take back into school,' I said. 'We're going to be rehearsing in the lunch breaks.' But Mum ignored me, and I knew better than to push it. To my relief, she put the letter on the side. At least it wasn't in the bin.

George kept me off school the next day. He was smirking when he told me, at breakfast, that I wouldn't be going. He had heard me telling Mum about the dance, and I was sure he did it on purpose, thinking I would miss out on the rehearsals and be dropped. I begged to go, but a chilling look from George soon silenced me. It seemed he wanted to teach me a lesson for being happy; it always seemed to annoy him and Mum if I was excited or looking forward to something.

As Tanya, Jamie and Paul left for school and Mum went off to work, I sat on the sofa, praying that he would change his mind and let me go, but he didn't. The door slammed and I sat in silence, wondering why it was just me he had kept at home. Until then, he'd always kept Tanya and Jamie as well. He used to try to keep Paul at home too, but Paul started refusing to stay. He defied George and walked out of the door.

He knew he'd get a beating, but he was hit so often that he seemed not to care any more. It was almost as though he was able to switch off the pain, or at least ignore it. That often made things worse for him, because Mum and George would try even harder to hurt him and make him cry. On many occasions they beat him with sticks and pieces of wood, attacking his legs and body.

The others had been gone for only a few minutes when I heard George call for me to go upstairs. Slowly, I got to my feet and made my way towards the stairs, dreading what was coming.

When I got to the landing, George wasn't waiting for me in his usual place. I looked around for him and saw the light was on in the bedroom he and Mum shared.

'In here.' His voice came from inside the room.

I walked, as slowly as I dared, towards the door.

George was standing next to the bed, naked except for a pair of socks. His eyes bored into me. I felt very scared. Something different was happening. But what?

'Take your clothes off and lie down on the bed,' he said.

I knew that if I asked why it would make him angry and he would hurt me even more.

I took off my t-shirt, skirt and knickers and left them on the floor. I looked over to the bed. There were pictures and magazines laid out on it, all with naked women on them. They looked like the women in the films George showed us.

George made me lie on the bed, next to the pictures. As I did, he began to rub his penis, while his eyes darted from one picture to another and then back to me.

I had never felt so scared in my whole life, but I couldn't make a noise. My heart was beating so fast and hard that I thought my chest was going to explode.

George came towards me and put his penis in my mouth, grabbing my hair as he did so, dragging my head back and forth slowly, and then fast, and then slow again.

'That's it, dust it nicely,' he said as he grabbed hold of my legs with his other hand. He was panting as he shoved my leg to one side and then pushed his big fingers inside me. He rammed them in deeper, then began pulling them in and out. The pain was excruciating. Tears rolled down the side of my face. I knew I mustn't cry out, but I was finding it harder and harder to stay quiet. I tried to think of something else – anything but what was actually happening to me.

After what seemed like a long time, George closed his eyes, grunted loudly and began to fire his sticky mess into my mouth, his knees buckling against the bed.

Then he straightened up, gathered his clothes and threw mine onto the bed, before picking up all the magazines and walking out of the room.

'Get some water from the bathroom if you want,' he called as he went downstairs.

I lay on the bed sobbing. If this was love, then why did it

hurt so much? Why did it make me feel sick and not special or loved at all?

Wiping my tears away with my hand, I pulled my clothes back on, not sure whether I was meant to go downstairs and sit with him or stay in my bedroom.

I crept into my room, hoping it wouldn't make George angry. I lay on the bed cuddling my little pepper doll. She had a soft body and hard plastic arms, legs and head, and I loved her more than any other toy I'd ever had. I called her Amber, after Amber Smith at school. She smelled nice, like the real Amber. I had got her for Christmas – in a little crib with a blanket – and it had been my best Christmas ever.

Lying on my bed, I thought about the May Day dance. 'Please let me do it,' I prayed. 'Don't let it be too late.' I thought that if I could make it as far as the performance then Mum and George could come and they'd have a reason to be proud of me. Then maybe Mum would love me and George wouldn't hurt me any more.

How could I get George to let me go to school? If he knew how much I wanted to go, he would stop me. Then I had an idea. I remembered the time George had made me go to school when I had my face covered in Gentian Violet. He didn't like me being at home if there was anything wrong with me, he didn't want the hassle of having to take care of me. So if I wanted to go to school, then I had to make George believe I was ill.

I thought hard about what I would have to do to convince him. I didn't want to get it wrong. If I did, I'd miss the dance and get a hiding too.

The day seemed to drag on. After an hour or so in my room, I went downstairs, afraid that if I was gone too long George would get angry. I sat on the sofa and stared at the TV, willing the hours to pass. When George told me to get myself something to eat, I said I wasn't hungry. It wasn't hard to pretend. After what George had done to me that morning, I really didn't feel like eating.

In the afternoon I asked if I could go and lie down, and George said yes, probably relieved to see the back of me. I waited until Mum and the other kids had come home, and then went slowly downstairs, holding my stomach and complaining that my tummy hurt and I felt sick.

I could see the agitation on Mum's face as she glanced towards George.

'Don't look at me,' he scowled. 'I've had to put up with the whingeing bitch all day, and I can tell you another thing: I won't be doing it tomorrow if she's still like this. She can go to bloody school and they can sort her out.'

I couldn't believe it. My plan was working. I looked towards Mum, trying to appear as pathetic as I could.

'You heard your dad, now stop your bloody moaning and crying, before I give you something to cry about.'

I turned and made my way out of the living room and

back upstairs. I was glad my act had worked so well, but I couldn't help wondering what I had done to make them both hate me so much.

The next morning, I said I still felt ill and George couldn't get me out of the door and off to school fast enough. Once I was out of sight of the house, I skipped the whole way.

For the rest of the week I pleaded every day to be kept at home and George looked disgusted and ordered me to school. In the lunch breaks the teacher taught us to dance around a beautifully decorated pole, covered in ribbons. I felt like a fairy, dancing in a magical garden.

The only problem was that I still hadn't brought my parental consent form back. Each time the teacher asked, I said I had forgotten it and would bring it in the next day. Luckily, she just smiled at me and let it go, raising her eyebrows in a funny way. But I couldn't ask Mum to sign it yet, as she and George thought I was still sick and would wonder how I had been dancing with an upset stomach.

I made it to four of the rehearsals. There was only one left, on the day before the performance, which was to be on a Wednesday afternoon. Even if George made me stay at home on the Tuesday, I knew the dance by heart and would be all right. But I had to have that signed letter, or I would miss the performance, and that would break my heart. And I had to persuade Mum and George to come and see me dance. I was sure that if they did, everything would get better.

Two days before the performance, the whole thing almost went up in smoke, when Tanya blurted out over tea that I was dancing on Wednesday at school. I sank into my seat, wishing I could vanish. I couldn't believe it. I looked up at Tanya, who immediately realised she had landed me in it. Now it was her turn to sink into her seat.

I sat playing with the peas on my plate, waiting for an outburst from Mum or George. But there was nothing. Either neither of them had heard Tanya, or they didn't care. I sat there, hardly daring to breathe, for the next five minutes.

After tea was finished, I hurried up to my room and Tanya followed soon after. I explained that I needed Mum or George to sign the form, and wanted them to come along and watch me perform. I could tell just by looking at Tanya that she didn't have much hope for me. She didn't need to say anything – the look in her eyes was enough.

The next day, I tried to pluck up the courage to ask Mum to sign the letter, but she was in a bad mood and I didn't dare. I shot out of the door, grateful to be able to make it for the final rehearsal.

On the day of the performance, I woke feeling excited, but scared too. I couldn't leave it any longer to ask Mum. What if she said no?

I went downstairs, careful not to look too cheerful, hoping that Mum would be in a good mood. She was in the kitchen, having a cup of coffee before work. Luckily, George was still upstairs. I went and got the letter from the mantelpiece in the living room, where it had sat all this time. Mum's face was hard to read as I approached her and put it down in front of her on the table. I had never wanted anything as much as this.

Mustering all my courage, my voice quavering, I said, 'This letter needs to be in today, Mum. It's for the May Day dance – I just need you to sign it so I can hand it in.'

Mum looked at the letter I had put down and began looking around the room. I dived over to the drawer where I had seen George go for pens when he wanted to do the crossword in the paper. I grabbed a pen and thrust it towards her, trying not to show my excitement.

'It starts at two o'clock and there are special seats right at the front for the mums and dads of the children taking part,' I announced proudly as she scribbled her name.

I grabbed the letter and shoved it into my pocket. 'Thanks, Mum. Please come, you're going to love it, we were practising all last week,' I blurted out. I stopped suddenly. Oh no! I had gone and ruined everything. Mum would realise I'd been pretending I was sick all week and, even worse, she would tell George.

Stricken, I waited for the explosion. But nothing happened. Mum's face seemed distant. Perhaps she hadn't heard me. I took a couple of steps backwards towards the door.

'That it?' she asked.

'Yes, thanks, Mum,' I said, and bolted out of the door,

grabbing my PE bag as I went. I was setting off much too early, and with no breakfast, but I didn't care – I was as high as a kite on a summer day.

I skipped all the way to school. I just couldn't stop smiling as I bobbed down the first alleyway and onto the street across from the school. There were only a few teachers about as I approached the main entrance, along with a boy who was always early as his mum was a teacher at the school.

'Hiya, Robert,' I yelled as I made my way up the path, grinning from ear to ear. He glanced over and then back at his feet, ignoring me as usual. But for once I didn't care. I was too happy.

I made my way through the school and into the infants' playground. It was strange being there all alone. I walked over to where I usually sat on the back wall, but then I realised I had the whole yard to myself. I could go anywhere. I spotted the white markings of the hopscotch area. At breaktime there were normally kids running all over it, or groups of girls hopscotching. I had never played, but I knew I could do it, as Tanya and I had practised on the street near home.

I ran over to the start and jumped on to the first square, dancing my way up and down, up and down, spinning round, trying to go faster and faster each time. It was so much fun. I wished I could play all the time, with the other girls. Suddenly I realised someone was watching me. I turned to see my teacher, smiling from the side door into the school.

'Make sure you save some of that energy for the dancing this afternoon, Louise, you want to put on a good show for your mum and dad,' she called. 'I hope you've brought your letter in.'

'I have, Miss, it's here,' I called back, pulling it out of my pocket and running to hand it over.

Morning lessons seemed to last for ever. Even the sums lesson I normally loved dragged on and on. All I could think about was the performance that afternoon. I went through the routine over and over again in my head.

I wasn't the only one who was excited. The others who were dancing seemed to have an extra bounce in their step too. Maddie Harris had had her hair cut into a little bob, and it was shining with sparkly hair gel. I put my hand up to my own hair. I had tried my best to brush it and get the knots out, but I knew it wasn't shiny and pretty like Maddie's.

When lunchtime arrived I was too excited and nervous to eat much, even though I'd had no breakfast. My insides were doing somersaults so badly that I was afraid I'd be sick. Then the bell went for the end of lunch and I made my way to my classroom with my PE bag. Most of the others were already there, chatting away to each other as Miss stood at the front of the class writing out on the board the order in which we would be lining up to walk out on stage.

There it was, clear as anything, up on the board for all to see; Louise Fox. I was to go out third from the end, between

Timmy and Sally. It was really happening. This was my chance. I was going to go out there and show everyone I wasn't different – I was just the same as them. And Mum and George would be so proud of me and smile at me as I danced.

I pulled out my PE clothes and plimsolls and began undressing as fast as I could. It wasn't until I was dressed that I noticed the other girls weren't in their PE kits. They had put on pink leotards and had fancy dance tights and leg-warmers, ballet shoes and ribbons in their hair. I looked like the boys, who had on t-shirts and shorts.

My face must have fallen, because the teacher came over to me.

'Let's get this in your hair, Louise,' she said softly, producing a pink ribbon. She brushed my hair into a ponytail, and tied the ribbon round it. 'There, you look lovely,' she said, smiling down at me. She reminded me of Amber's mum, who had spoken so nicely to me and looked so welcoming and warm.

'Right, get ready everyone – get yourselves in order – we're going out now. Good luck, and don't forget to smile,' said the teacher.

I looked down at my feet and wriggled my toes around, hoping I would remember what to do. The teacher led the way down the corridor and across to the main hall, turning back every now and then to smile at us. When we got to the stage she stepped to the side, touching each of us as we went past her, whispering good luck or just giving us a big smile.

As I went up I could see parents waving to their sons and daughters on stage. I was trying to find Mum and George, to give them a big smile and wave, like everyone else, but I couldn't see them. I searched up and down the rows several times before I understood that they weren't there.

My heart sank. I had wanted so much for them to come. I should have known they wouldn't, because they had never been to anything at school. But somehow I had wanted to believe that this time was different, that just this one time they would come.

Shoulders sagging, I turned to take my place for the dance. Then, out of the corner of my eye, I spotted someone waving. I looked across and saw Amber's mum, waving at me and smiling. I smiled back and gave her a wave. Someone was watching me after all.

We positioned ourselves around the maypole. It was beautifully decorated with pink ribbons. We took hold of one each, and began.

For the next twenty minutes I was a different person. I wasn't the shy, quiet little girl with no friends. I was popular, confident, happy and pretty. If I could have captured that feeling and bottled it I would have. Then I could have kept it in a secret place and taken it out whenever I felt low or sad, just to remember how wonderful it was.

At the end, when I stood with the others and we bowed as the parents applauded and cheered, I felt I would burst with joy. Amber's mum was still smiling at me, and I smiled back. She couldn't have known how much she did for me that day, but I never forgot it.

Chapter Four

After that first time, George often made me go into his and Mum's room and lie on the bed while he did horrible things to me with his fingers and made me do the dusting with him. He always had the pictures of naked women laid out on the bed. And sometimes he would leave the curtains open, so that if anyone in the houses opposite had glanced over, they would have seen what he was doing.

He would force me to go upstairs with him two or even three or four times a week. Tanya and Jamie had to go upstairs with him too. And all three of us would come down again with tears in our eyes, subdued and unhappy.

When it was my turn, I learned to block out most of what was happening. I would count, or try rolling my eyes back in my head, or stare at the ceiling and try to imagine I was somewhere else. I got so good at switching off that as soon as George started on me, a kind of shutter would come down in my mind and I would only be half aware of what he was doing. It didn't make the pain or the hurt or the sadness any less, but it got me through it.

I became very scared of the dark, but Mum and George

just thought it was funny. One night I was up in the loo when George turned all the lights off, for a laugh. I was left in the pitch black, absolutely terrified. I called out, but no-one came, so I began to make my way downstairs, hanging onto the banister and going very slowly, almost paralysed by fear. As I got to the bottom, I saw a huge black shadow through the glass panel in our front door. It was too much for me; I began screaming and sobbing. George and Mum put the lights back on and came out of the living room to answer the front door. It turned out to be the husband of Mum's sister. I was left shaking like a leaf, but Mum and George thought it was hilarious. After that, I was even more frightened and couldn't be alone with the lights off for many years.

The only time Mum was kind to me was in front of other people. A couple of times she had to take me to hospital, and then she would suddenly be the kind and sympathetic mother I yearned for. One time, I fell over and banged my head on the sideboard. I had a bad cut, which was pouring blood, so Mum took me to the local accident and emergency unit. We had to wait ages, and Mum was so nice to me – even offering me sweets – that I didn't mind the pain; it was worth it for that hour or two of mothering.

Another time, I had to go into hospital to have grommets put into my ears, because I wasn't hearing much and the doctors said I had glue ear – fluid in the middle ear. It's a common procedure that hundreds of kids have done, but it still felt a bit scary to me, having to be in hospital overnight. Mum was so nice to me in front of the nurses that I wondered if someone had swapped her in the night for a different mum who looked the same. But once we got home she lost interest in me, and things carried on just the same as before.

By the time I turned six, Mum had given up her job, so we had even less money. And with all that time on her hands, she started spending hours poring over jigsaw puzzles on a board in the living room. She chose incredibly complex 1000- piece jigsaws, and would painstakingly put the pieces together over several weeks, oblivious to the rest of us as she munched chocolate and squinted at the hundreds of tiny bits of cardboard. When she'd finally finished one she would frame it and hang it on the wall.

The other thing she liked to do, from time to time, was bake. She would make batches of buns and the whole house would fill with the delicious smell of hot dough. We would be allowed to have one after tea, and they were lovely. But one was all we got, because Mum would eat the rest, one after another, as she sat watching her favourite soaps.

I thought that I would have to live with George forever. The beatings and abuse went on and on and I couldn't imagine things getting better.

And then one day, not long before I turned seven, everything changed.

It happened on a day when George had decided to pay a rare weekday visit to his mum. After tea, Mum settled down on the floor, her feet up on the settee, and ordered me to tickle them with a cotton bud, and rub foot cream into them. While I rubbed away, Mum stared at the TV, her glasses perched on the end of her nose, eating her way through a large bar of chocolate. I looked longingly at it, but she was oblivious to me, and I didn't dare ask her for a piece, knowing that I would either be totally ignored or get a furious look and a threat of trouble from George when he got home.

Tanya was sitting beside me, waiting for her turn with Mum's feet, and both Paul and Jamie were playing out in the street.

Suddenly, there was a furious knocking at the door. Mum told Tanya to answer, and Auntie Coleen burst in, sobbing and calling Mum's name. Auntie Coleen was one of Mum's sisters. The two of them were close, and often saw one another, and we sometimes went to play with Auntie Coleen's daughter, Emma, who was a little bit older than Tanya.

Auntie Coleen and Mum hurried off into the kitchen, slamming the door behind them as they went. Tanya and I looked at each other, both of us confused and alarmed. We could hear murmurs and then raised voices coming from the kitchen. Neither of us spoke, but we knew something was seriously wrong.

A few minutes later, Auntie Coleen came out, followed by Mum.

'Right, you two, I want you to listen carefully,' Auntie Coleen said. Her tone was very serious and my mind was racing. What had I done wrong? Had the shopkeeper on our street seen me stealing biscuits? Had George told her I hadn't been a good girl? I glanced over at Tanya who was looking down at the floor.

'Emma stayed at her friend's house last night and while she was there her friend's dad tried to do something to her,' Auntie Coleen said.

The hairs on my arms stood on end and my insides twisted into knots. What was this about?

'Do you know what I'm saying?' she went on. 'He tried to touch her in rude places.'

For a moment there was silence as she looked over at Mum, who looked nervous.

'Has anyone done that to you?' Mum asked, her voice quieter than usual. 'Has anyone touched you?'

I felt panicky. What did she mean? Was it what George did to us? I thought Mum knew all about that, I thought it was what all families did.

My heart was beating very fast and my eyes switched from the floor to Tanya and back to the floor again. Unsure about whether to say anything or not, I shook my head and swallowed hard. Tanya did the same.

Auntie Coleen came over to us and leaned down. 'Don't worry,' she said. 'You won't get into trouble. Just tell us the truth – has anyone touched you in private places?'

There was silence for a moment, and then Tanya spoke.

'Yeah, but only Dad,' she said, eyes fixed to the floor.

'Me too,' I added quickly.

Mum shrieked, startling us. She started shouting at Auntie Coleen, but I couldn't make out what she was saying. I felt very scared. What was happening? Why was she so upset? Were we in trouble? Tanya had said it was only Dad, and that was OK wasn't it?

Auntie Coleen grabbed hold of Mum, who was sobbing loudly, and held her tight. Tanya and I stood rooted to the spot, watching them. I looked over to my sister, wanting reassurance, wanting this to end.

Auntie Coleen let go of Mum, who ran into the kitchen, grabbing hold of the phone on the way. Auntie Coleen reached out her hands and pulled us towards her. By this time I was shaking and it was so good to be held tightly in her arms. I hoped she would never let go, but a moment later Mum came out of the kitchen and Auntie Coleen let go of us and went over to her.

Still unsure about what to do, Tanya and I stood silently, confused and scared, watching the madness unfold. Why was Mum crying so much? We just didn't understand.

The phone rang and Mum picked it up.

'You bastard, what have you done, George?' she yelled. 'Don't go anywhere, they're coming for you,' she shouted, and she slammed the phone down.

Mum turned to look at me and Tanya, but without connecting or focusing on us. It felt as though she was looking straight through us, as if we were not really there. That's how it felt inside as well.

For the next half hour, Mum paced up and down, crying and saying to Auntie Coleen, 'What if he comes here? If he does, that'll be it. Make sure the chain's on the door.'

Mum and Auntie Coleen carried on talking to one another, while Tanya and I stayed where we were. We had no idea what to do. It seemed like Mum hadn't known about what George was doing – she was in a dreadful state. And it wasn't OK, like George had said. It was wrong, because Mum had called the police and shouted at George.

Now George knew we had told he would get us, I was sure. Thinking about the beating we would get, I started to cry.

Suddenly there was a bang on the door. We all jumped. Then a voice said, 'It's the police,' and Auntie Coleen opened the door. Two officers came in, a man and a woman. The man went into the kitchen with Mum and Auntie Coleen, while the woman officer came and sat with us, smiling awkwardly at us both, but not saying anything.

When they all came back out of the kitchen, the police officers said we needed to go to the police station. They took us all outside and put us into their car. No-one spoke for the whole journey. Tanya and I sat in the back, our heads down, looking at the floor. What had we done? What was going to happen now?

When we arrived, Auntie Coleen put her arm around Mum as we were taken to a door at the back of the station. The lady officer gently ushered me and Tanya inside, walking between us with a hand on each of our shoulders. We were all taken into a room and asked to sit down, and a few minutes later another woman appeared. She was small and round, with glasses and wavy brown hair and she told us her name was Anna Smithson and she was from the social services. I wondered what they were.

Mum and Tanya were asked to go into another room, while Auntie Coleen and I stayed where we were. The lady officer brought in some orange juice and a plate of biscuits and showed me a box of toys and books in the corner of the room, saying I was welcome to play with them. Her voice was gentle and that made me feel a bit better. I was grateful for the drink because my mouth felt so dry, but I didn't feel like playing. I wanted to know what was happening, but I was too scared to ask anyone and no-one seemed to want to tell me.

It seemed like hours before Tanya came back, and when she did it was my turn to disappear with Mum into the other little room. Inside were a man and a woman sitting on one side of a table. I didn't know if they were police officers or not, as they didn't have uniforms on. We were asked to sit in the two chairs facing them, on the other side, while the lady from social services, Anna, sat nearby. She smiled at me reassuringly and that made me feel a tiny bit less scared.

'Hello, Louise, me and my colleague are just going to ask you a few questions,' the woman said, leaning towards me. 'There's nothing to be worried about, we just want you to tell us as much as you know.'

Mum was sitting next to me and I looked at her. I hoped she would nod or smile to let me know it was OK, but she was looking down at the table with her head in her hands.

Slowly and falteringly, I began to describe what George had done. Whenever I stopped they asked questions in nice, soft voices and, feeling encouraged, I was soon in full flow, telling them everything. In a funny sort of way, I liked the attention they were giving me. They kept saying I was doing well and to keep going, and that felt nice.

Next, they handed me a pencil and paper and asked me to draw pictures of what had happened and where I was and where George was when we did the dusting. I did my best and when I had finished I looked up and saw that the woman looked upset. I looked over at the man, and he looked very solemn. There wasn't a warm feeling in the room any more and I burst into tears and turned to Mum, who turned away from me. What had I done that was so wrong that all these people, including my mum, looked so upset and angry? I felt so empty and alone, even though there were four grown-ups there with me.

The two officers got up from their chairs and nodded towards the woman from social services. She quickly stood and, touching my back, ushered me out of the interview room and into the room where Tanya and Auntie Coleen were. Mum followed and a few minutes later we were told that we could go home. We were given a lift back in the police car.

Paul and Jamie, who'd been out when the police first came, had been found and taken to the police station as well. They arrived back home soon after us, both of them looking upset.

When we got home there was an angry silence. Mum didn't cuddle us or reassure us and she didn't make any tea for us – but I don't think I could have eaten anyway. I felt awful, as though we had spoilt everything, we were the ones in the wrong and it was all our fault. I felt sick inside, my head was spinning and I was finding it hard to focus on anything at all.

The police had told us that George had been arrested and we wouldn't have to see him again, but we were all still scared that he would come back to the house and find us and then punish us for telling. Every time we heard a sound outside the door we all jumped.

That night, lying in bed, I felt the whole world had come to an end. I should have been happy that George wasn't around any more and couldn't hurt us, but I wasn't. I was afraid that Mum would never forgive us – she seemed so angry. I felt alone and cold and unable to sleep. I wanted to speak to Tanya but didn't know how to. It was as if there was some kind of unwritten rule that we must never speak about it.

The following day, we were all driven into the centre of Manchester by a lady from social services. We were taken to a big building which we were told was called a medical centre, where there were doctors. When we arrived, Anna Smithson was there. She explained that a doctor was just going to check us over, to make sure that we were all right, and no damage had been done.

We were introduced to a lady doctor who was a lot older than Anna and not as nice as some of the other people who had helped us before.

The next forty-five minutes were a nightmare. The doctor took me into a small room, while Anna stayed with the others in the waiting area. Mum came with me, and she sat in a chair against the wall. There was a nurse there too, and she led me over to a high bed on one side of the room. I was asked to take off my trousers and knickers, before the doctor helped me up onto the bed. The doctor parted my legs and began to examine me, prodding and poking and sticking instruments inside me, scraping bits out and putting swabs onto small bits of plastic. The pain was almost unbearable, as she opened my legs further and further. It felt as though my insides were torn and cut, and she was making it all worse.

I cried the whole time and I kept looking over at Mum. I

wished she would come over and hold my hand or smile at me, and tell me it would all be over soon, but she stayed in her chair and didn't even look at me. The nurse was trying to calm me down, asking me about school and all sorts of other things that didn't make sense to me, while holding my legs open with a tight grip on each knee. The doctor also ignored my tears; she didn't look sympathetic at all, going about her duties in a very robotic way, as though I wasn't actually a real child, but a toy that she was checking to see if everything worked.

When they finally finished, I was allowed to put my clothes back on. The nurse opened the door for me to go out, and ushered Jamie in next. His face was white and scared. Wiping my tears on my sleeve, I looked up at him quickly and then back down to the floor, before the door shut behind me.

Back in the waiting area, Anna put her arm around my shoulders and led me over to a chair next to her, telling me the worst was over now. If only that had been true. The test results would later show that Tanya, Jamie and I had all been sexually abused, though Paul had not. Jamie had been anally raped and had internal tears and infections, while Tanya and I had to have antibiotics and cream for the internal damage done to us.

We all came home subdued and shaken. But once again Mum said nothing to us, and over the following days she behaved as though nothing had happened at all. She went back to lying on the floor with her feet on the sofa, eating chocolate, and we all carried on as normal. She only referred to what had happened once, asking me and Tanya why we hadn't said no to George, and why we hadn't told her about it. We didn't know what to say. She had always known how frightened of George we were.

I often wished that Mum would give me a cuddle and tell me that she loved me, or that she was glad nasty George had gone away, or that everything would be all right. But, if anything, the opposite happened – Mum was very distant and irritable and often made us feel that it was our fault George wasn't with us any more. When we didn't have something, or needed some food or money, she would say, 'Now George isn't here' and look at us in a way that made us feel it was our fault he was gone. She often cried and said she missed him, and we all felt guilty for sending him away.

Looking back, I've wondered why Mum chose that moment to ask us if we'd been abused. Her sister had come round worried sick because something had happened to her daughter. Yet instead of supporting her and making sure Auntie Coleen and Emma were all right, Mum switched the focus to herself and her family. I've wondered, many times, whether she knew what George was doing, and chose that moment to expose it simply to go one better than her sister. If Auntie Coleen had a child who'd been molested, well, Mum could produce three, with a far worse story. It sounds bizarre, but it fits in with all Mum's bizarre behaviour. She didn't know how to really sympathise with another person; her only aim was to go one better. Whether or not this was what prompted her to ask us and to expose George, Mum seemed to regret it and blame us once he was gone.

Over the next few weeks, school was the only place where I was able to forget about what had happened and the trouble I felt I had caused – just for a little while. But although we went more than we had when George was there, Mum often kept us at home if she felt lonely, even though she didn't talk to us much and would send us out to play.

The fear we'd felt around George had been replaced by uncertainty and fear of a different kind. None of us knew how to be around Mum, and even around other people. We knew we were the reason why George wasn't there and Mum was always upset. We walked around silently, trying not to upset her any further. Sometimes she was so distant that she would only say 'yes', 'no' or 'I don't know' to us for days at a time, and it scared us. We didn't know how to make her feel better or put things right.

And to make things even worse, even though George wasn't in the house any more, he was still in our lives. He was in prison, awaiting trial, and the worst thing of all for us was that Mum insisted we all visit him every week. We'd travel across the city on the bus and then queue outside the prison with the other visitors. Inside there were metal gates, warders in uniforms and bars on all the windows. I hated it. We'd be searched and then sent into the large visiting room, where men sat at little tables with chairs around them.

George would be sitting at one of the tables, wearing jeans and a jumper with what looked to me like a red netball bib over the top, as though he was in a sports team. It was very odd seeing him out of his usual neatly ironed shirts and trousers, and even odder to see him seemingly calm and relaxed.

Mum would make a big fuss of him, while the four of us sat beside her, and then, at her insistence, Tanya and I had to sit on George's knee and tell him we missed him and loved him and wanted him back home. I would have given anything not to have to do it, but Mum had told us it would make her happy, and I wanted to please her. I was also afraid that George would soon be back at home – Mum kept saying that he would – and I was afraid that if I said no, he might be even angrier with me than I imagined he already was.

The whole thing made me feel so uncertain. The police and Anna Smithson had told us George had done wrong and that we wouldn't have to see him again – yet now Mum was asking us to sit on his knee. It seemed that what they had said was all lies and I felt even more stupid and bad for telling.

All around us other prisoners sat with their families, some not saying anything, others shouting and screaming and crying at each other. I used to look around and wonder what all these people had done. Were they in prison because they had done the same thing as George?

I was always so relieved to get out of the prison and go home. But that wasn't the end of it. Between prison visits, Mum made us sit down at the living-room table and write letters to him, telling him how much we loved and missed him and that we couldn't wait till he was back home with us again.

She told us that he had admitted everything and was going to plead guilty so that we wouldn't have to be interviewed over and over again and appear in court to testify against him. He did it for us because he still loved us, she said. I found it hard to believe that this was true. He didn't show the least sign of loving us, and never had. But I would never have dared to say this to Mum.

It's far more likely that his lawyer advised him that the evidence against him was damning and told him he would get a lighter sentence if he pleaded guilty. And making us sit on his knee in the prison was her attempt to show the authorities that he was really a loving dad who'd just made a slip-up.

It all left me very confused. I didn't know who was actually in the wrong. Was it me, because I didn't say no to George and fight him off, and because I told on him? Or was it him? I didn't know, and having to write to him, and then sit on his knee as Mum smiled and chatted with him only confused me more. But our visits came to an abrupt end after several months, when George went to court. He was given a four-year sentence and sent to a prison at the other end of the country.

Chapter Five

Mum took it badly when George was sent down. She had really believed he would be let off, and had told us he would be coming home.

After he was sentenced, she cried a lot and said she wouldn't be able to go and see him, as the prison he'd been sent to was too far away. Then, one day, while we were at school, she slashed her wrists.

We didn't know about it until we got in from school. Nanna was there and she told us Mum was in hospital and had nearly died. I was terrified. What would I do if Mum died? And why would she want to die? I knew it must be because she wanted George back, and it was my and Tanya's fault that he was gone. I felt so bad and guilty and worried that I couldn't sleep that night, even though Nanna had said that Mum would be all right and would be coming home in the morning. I didn't know then that Mum's cuts were only superficial, and she had phoned for help as soon as she'd cut herself.

Mum did come home, and we stayed off school so that we could see her. She looked pale and lay on the sofa with big white bandages over her wrists. We made her cups of tea and rubbed her feet and tried to make her feel better.

Mum did seem to feel better, very quickly, because after that day she hardly ever mentioned George again and she began to behave as though he had never existed. She started asking her eldest sister, Auntie Carol, over a lot. Nanna came too, and the three of them would sit for hours playing card games like crash and cribbage. They ignored us, except when they wanted a cup of tea or a buttie – then they'd ask me to make it.

They got so engrossed in their card games that they often told us to make our own tea, or go to the fish shop and get some chips. They'd tell us to get out of the house and go outside and play. Tanya would run off with her friends and I would wander about looking for someone to hang about with. Carol's house was nearby and she had three children, but they were all younger than me and they were told to stay in their garden. So sometimes I'd stand outside their gate and talk to them. But mostly I was alone.

After George had gone to prison, some of the neighbours had jeered at Mum, saying that he'd got what he deserved and calling her names. Mum would go round to their houses brandishing a stick and stand outside shouting, 'Come on then!' We used to be so embarrassed we'd stay indoors, giggling nervously and hoping she'd give up and come back home. It got so bad that other kids on the estate would pick on us because of Mum. They said she was mad, and we must be mad too.

Even though I knew he'd been locked away, it took a long time before I began to believe that George really was gone. At first I didn't dare to believe it. I thought Mum would still make us visit him, or write. And I was afraid that he would find a way to get out of prison and come back, and then punish me for telling. But as the weeks went past and there was no sign of him, I gradually stopped watching out for him.

One thing made me very sad. Soon after George went to prison, his mum, Nanna Gladice, died. I missed her – she'd been one of the very few people who were kind to me, and I was sorry that she was gone.

I was still quiet in school, often daydreaming my way through classes and retreating to the wall in the playground. And at home things were better without George, but Mum wasn't an easy parent. Jamie, who was plump and dark-haired, and Tanya, who was slim and pretty with shiny brown hair and blue eyes, were her favourites. I got shouted at and hit far more often than them – though Mum didn't use a leather belt like George had, so it didn't hurt nearly as much. But for Paul, especially, life was still very tough. Blond-haired and skinny as a whippet, he slunk around the house, trying to avoid Mum's wrath, and stayed away as often as he could. She used to trap him in the gap at the end of the bunk-beds in his room, and she beat him so hard and so often that I once heard him begging for his life. She kept a pool cue in the house, even though none of us ever played pool. It was what she used to beat Paul with.

All the rules George had imposed went out of the window with Mum in charge. She couldn't be bothered with any of them. We had tea when she felt like making it and the house became a total tip, with mess everywhere. Every now and then she'd decide to have a big clean-up, then she'd let it go again and the mess would pile up. We didn't have set bedtimes any more; we stayed up until we were tired. Mum would let us stay up late and watch adult films like *A Nightmare on Elm Street*, which had an 18 certificate. I was seven when it first came out on video. Of course, it scared me witless. Afterwards, Jamie played tricks on me when I was going to bed, jumping out from behind doors in the dark, with clothes pegs on his fingers to make them look long and scary. I screamed my head off, but they all just thought it was funny.

There were bonuses though. In the mornings before school we were allowed to have the radio on – we loved that, because George had never permitted it. Mum used to make a big pan of porridge every morning, and every single day she burned it.

We all had problems. Jamie was still wetting the bed, and although it happened less often after George left, he still stank of urine all the time, and so did his bed.

Tanya had a nervous habit of biting the knuckle of her first finger – it was always in her mouth. And she would repeat things people said to her, but silently, mouthing the words. As for me, I constantly played with my hair, running it between my fingers, while going off into a world of my own, so that I didn't notice anything going on around me.

With Mum not working and George gone, money was tight. Mum went to social services almost every week, begging for handouts. We dressed in tatty, sometimes ragged and usually grubby clothes. There was no money for extras and we lived on a diet of egg and chips. Mum did make an effort sometimes – she knitted us all big chunky jumpers in the winter. We had a picture taken of the four of us wearing them – mine had a pink and white spotted pattern and was a bit tight. Paul's was spotted too, while Jamie and Tanya had green jumpers with a pattern of stripes on them. In the picture, we're standing in a row and Tanya and I have our hair tied back so tightly that we look as though it hurts.

There was another change after George went – social services became part of our lives. The person who came most often was Anna Smithson, who would visit us about once a month. I grew to like Anna. She had soft hands and kind-looking eyes, and she was always nicely dressed and had a smile for all of us.

Mum's reaction to the visits varied, depending on her mood. Occasionally she was all smiles, and we'd sit around the table and chat and Mum would say how well we were all doing.

But more often Mum would lose it, shouting and swearing at Anna, yelling a stream of obscenities, while us children cringed in the next room.

Sometimes Anna couldn't even get in through the door. Mum would ignore the bell and tell us all to hide, or we would all go out when she was due to come round. Or Mum would shout at her from the living room to 'Fuck off and leave us alone'. Anna would leave, but she always came back, and despite Mum's appalling behaviour, she was always nice to us and polite.

As well as Anna's visits to us, we had to go to the social services offices once a month for family therapy sessions. We'd all have to sit and talk with Anna or another social worker, and sometimes they talked to each of us alone for a few minutes, just to ask if everything was OK. We always said it was.

Life seemed to be settling down, and if it wasn't great, then it was certainly better than it had been.

And then Terry arrived.

I didn't notice him move in across the road, but it wasn't long after George was sent to prison. He was in his late forties, stocky, with a shaved head. He wore grubby jumpers and a big belt tied round his trousers, which were pulled up high over his hips.

Terry lived alone, so it was odd that he'd been given a three-bedroom house. He did have a grown-up son who visited from time to time, so perhaps that was why. He also had a dog that went everywhere with him – an old mongrel called Barney. I loved Barney; he would always come up to me to be petted when he saw me in the street. I would stroke him gently under his chin and he loved it when I tickled him.

I never knew what Terry's job was, but he seemed to work funny hours and was often around during the day, usually walking Barney. He seemed to be a bit of a loner, because apart from his son no-one ever visited his house. But he was always very friendly when he saw us playing outside. He would smile and let me play with Barney for a while before he went back home.

Mum soon got talking to Terry. She had alienated so many neighbours that there weren't many people who would pass the time of day with her, so she homed in on someone new. She asked him over, and before long Terry was round at our house most days. He would bring cans of beer for Mum and she would make his tea for him after work. He was a bit of a replacement for George, although he and Mum were just friends. They would sit and chat together over cups of tea and when he offered to babysit for us while Mum went to bingo or round to see one of her sisters, she was delighted.

Terry made us all feel special by talking to us and taking a real interest. We kids all liked him and we were glad that he seemed to make Mum happy, because if she was in a good mood we wouldn't bear the brunt of her bad temper. So when he offered to have me and Tanya over at his house for a bit, we all thought it was a good idea. Mum jumped at the chance to let someone else have us. We often seemed to irritate her and she was always looking for ways to get rid of us, so she didn't ask too many questions.

Terry's house was pretty horrible. There was no carpet on the floor or the stairs, and the walls were bare and undecorated. The kitchen was filthy and stank because Barney peed on the floor. And the battered furniture was covered in dog hairs. On top of the dirt, the place stank of the Old Spice aftershave that he wore all the time. But Tanya and I didn't really mind any of this, because we had fun with Terry. He'd buy us treats and get videos for us to watch and we had a much better time than we had at home.

It seemed a bit odd that Terry used to lock the front door once we got inside, putting the key on a shelf out of our reach, but we weren't worried, because he was our friend.

Before long, the two of us began going over to Terry's almost every day, while Mum played cards with Nanna and Auntie Carol or one of her other sisters, Auntie Colleen or Auntie Claire. I was glad to be out of the house, because when I was there Mum was forever ordering me to make cups of tea and chip butties for everyone. I cooked and cleaned and ran around doing all the housework, while they made jokes about me being slow or ugly or stupid. I never felt wanted or included, so going to Terry's house was a bit of a treat.

For some reason, Tanya didn't have to do as much as I did at home. Probably because she wasn't too afraid to say no, and she would walk out of the house and go and play rather than cook and clean. But she was still glad to get away. Mum made it clear that she didn't want any of us around, so when Paul and Jamie went off with their mates, Tanya and I headed over to Terry's.

Mum would tell us to make his tea so it would be ready for when he got home. We would go and put on the chips, eggs and peas and when Terry got back he would often have a present for us. He would bring back teddy bears and toys and even though he didn't go over to Mum's that much any more, he would still buy her food and even clothes. It seemed as if all she needed to do was snap her fingers and he would do whatever she wanted.

I thought Mum must have some magic hold over Terry. I didn't understand that Terry was currying favour with Mum to get to us girls, and buying affection from me and Tanya with his gifts.

Then Mum threatened to kill herself again. This time she locked the doors, so no-one could get into the house. Tanya and I were playing outside when Paul came running to tell us that Mum was locked in the house with a razor blade, threatening to slash her wrists again. He had seen the blade before

Mum closed the curtains, so that no-one could tell if she'd used it or not. We didn't know what to do – so we ran over to Terry's house. He was in bed after a night shift, but he got up and came over. We were all hysterical and crying, but Terry managed to get the back door open and went in and found Mum, who hadn't cut herself and was fine.

After that, we thought Terry was a hero, and we relied on him more than ever. Soon Tanya and I were spending more time with him than we were at home, so when he suggested that next time Mum went to bingo Tanya and I stay the night at his house, instead of him coming over to us, Mum readily agreed.

Tanya and I were only too happy. We thought it would be an adventure and we ran to get our nightdresses and tooth-brushes. We went over as usual, just before tea time, and Terry brought us fish and chips, which was a real treat. We all sat in the front room together eating them, and Terry told us we were going to have a great time and if we wanted we could make it a regular thing.

We agreed it would be great, both of us grinning and excited because it made us feel a bit special. We spent the evening watching television and laughing and joking, although Terry was very edgy about when we should be going to bed. Finally he decided it was time and told us both that our night-ies were upstairs in his room.

He explained that I would be sleeping downstairs on the

couch and Tanya would be in the spare room. I couldn't understand why I was downstairs, because I knew there was another empty bedroom. But I felt it would be rude to ask, so Tanya and I scampered upstairs and got ready for bed, and she went into her room, while I went back down to the living room. Terry handed me a quilt, said goodnight and then made his way up the stairs, turning the lights off as he went.

It was cold and I struggled to get comfortable as I tossed and turned, curled up in a ball. The only light I could see seeped in through the sides of the front door, from the street lamps outside. I wondered if Tanya had got to sleep and wished that I could be up there with her. We often got into the same bed at home, just to be close and to keep warm. It was comforting; I felt safer when I was with Tanya.

No matter how hard I tried, I just couldn't get to sleep. Although I was happy to be at Terry's, I was a little scared, downstairs on my own. So I was still awake when I saw a shadow in the hall, and heard soft footsteps. I was frightened, until I realised it was Terry. He came in and sat on the couch near my feet, resting his hand on my leg on top of the quilt.

'You OK, Louise?' he whispered.

'Yeah,' I whispered back.

His hand slipped under the quilt and onto my leg, gently holding and stroking it. It felt nice at first, but as his hand moved upwards to rest on my stomach I began to feel uncomfortable. His hand moved back down to my legs, which were curled up, and pulled them straight. Then he slid his head under the quilt. I could feel his hands running over me, stroking and rubbing me up and down.

I froze. I couldn't move. I couldn't speak.

I wanted to say something, but I didn't know how. I could feel his head between my legs and then a burning, painful sensation as his fingers entered me and began moving around inside me. I was in turmoil. Why was Terry doing the things that George had done?

I didn't want Terry to go to prison like George. Mum liked him, and she was nicer to us when he was around. Tanya and I liked him. Jamie liked him. He bought us presents, made Mum happier, made us laugh, gave us sweets, and gave me the one thing that I craved – attention.

So I lay silent, trying to pretend I was somewhere else, as Terry pushed his tongue into me, licking me and prodding at me with his fingers. It was probably only a few minutes, but it felt like hours until he finally stopped. Then he got up and walked off, without saying anything, leaving me in the darkness, alone, scared and confused. It was a long time before I managed to get to sleep.

The next morning, Terry and Tanya came down the stairs together, both looking cheerful. I looked towards Tanya to try to catch her eye, wondering if Terry had been to see her in the night too, but she was drifting off into the kitchen to get some breakfast.

'What do you want for breakfast, Louise?' Terry called, smiling at me over his shoulder.

'Anything,' I called back, trying hard to sound as though I was fine. I didn't want Terry to think I didn't like him, so I jumped up out of bed and joined them in the kitchen and the three of us had toast and cereal as though nothing at all had happened.

After that, we began staying the night at Terry's at least once or twice a week. And every time, Terry made me sleep downstairs, then appeared in the night and repeated what had happened that first night. Every time I lay awake, filled with dread, hoping he wouldn't come. But he always did.

I didn't know whether Terry was doing the same things to Tanya that he was doing to me. I wanted to ask her, but I didn't know how. It wasn't until I went up to the bathroom one morning and, through the open bedroom door, saw Tanya in Terry's bed that I realised it must be happening to her too. Terry shot across the room to close the door, but I had seen. Later I was to learn that he was not only doing the same to her, but that Tanya was actually sleeping in the same bed as him most nights that we stayed with him.

Despite the misery of those nights, I carried on going to his house, because I knew it was what everyone wanted. Mum and Terry both liked the arrangement and I didn't want to upset things. I told myself that at least Terry was nice to us. He got films for us to watch – his favourite was *Dirty Danc-*

ing; he said it made him feel nice. And he gave us all kinds of gifts and presents. At first we used to get toys and sweets. But as the weeks went past, the presents for me and Tanya changed. Terry stopped bringing us teddy bears and dolls and began buying clothes and make-up and taking us to have our hair done. On one occasion he took Tanya to the hairdresser and she came back with her hair permed. Mum loved it and said she looked so grown-up.

We both loved having new clothes instead of the hand-me-down tracksuit bottoms and t-shirts we were used to. Terry bought us short little tops that showed off our bellies and short skirts. We had clean white socks instead of the old dirty knee socks we had been used to. Terry even took us both shopping for bras, although at seven and ten we certainly didn't need them.

Tanya was his favourite and he showered her with gifts. We both spent a great deal of time at his house, it was our second home, and because of this, and the gifts, I felt I had to keep quiet about his night-time visits to me. I couldn't spoil it for everyone; Mum would hate me, and I was afraid Tanya would too. And in a funny way I even liked the attention Terry gave me. I told myself that he might buy Tanya chocolates and loads of gifts, but it was me he loved because he came down to see me at night when she was asleep. I was so starved of affection and my mind had been so twisted that I had no idea what was right or wrong or normal. I didn't know any different. I thought this was happening to all little girls – not just me. After all, Mum wanted us to be over there, so it had to be OK. And we wanted to please Mum, so even when I began to feel I'd rather not go to Terry's, I went anyway.

We were still having visits from Anna and going to family therapy sessions, and Mum decided that as Terry was now around so much, he should come too. She told social services that Terry was part of the family and that he should be involved, and when they refused she argued with Anna about it. The next time we went, she brought Terry anyway. He came in and sat down with all of us and there wasn't much Anna could do, though she did ask him to leave the room while she asked us some questions.

A few months after Terry moved in across the road, Mum started seeing a new boyfriend. She'd had a few passing boyfriends over the months, but this one seemed more serious. His name was John, and Mum was really smitten. He seemed nice, though we didn't see much of him; he always seemed to come round while we were at school, or out playing, or over at Terry's. Terry and Mum were as friendly as ever, he didn't seem bothered about her having a boyfriend. The only thing that changed was that we spent more time than ever over at his house, because it gave Mum a chance to be with John.

By the time Mum had known him for four months she was talking about getting married. I hated the idea of someone else moving in – it was nicer with just Mum and us. And John had two children of his own, who lived with him – I couldn't see how we'd all fit in.

One day Anna Smithson called on us. She made it through the front door and was in the kitchen with Mum while we were in the front room watching television. Anna explained to Mum that one of the neighbours had made calls to social services about Tanya and me and our frequent visits over to see Terry, and had said that he was developing an inappropriate relationship with us.

Mum refused to have any of it. She opened the back door and shouted, 'The neighbours want to mind their bloody business.' Then she marched out through the hall and opened the front door, nodding at Anna to leave. Anna, realising that Mum was about to erupt, was out of the door in a flash. Mum slammed the door behind her and stomped off into the kitchen, cursing under her breath. She didn't want anyone interfering with her arrangements with Terry. She wasn't interested in what might be going on, she just wanted the goodies that Terry still showered on her. She certainly wasn't about to let some know-all from social services spoil the fun.

Several times after this, Anna raised concerns about Terry's relationship with us. She would ask us about it, but we always looked at Mum before we answered, aware that we mustn't say the wrong thing. We didn't want to upset her and get into trouble, and we trusted her too. If she said it was OK, then it must be. We heard Anna advising Mum, over and over again, to stop us going to Terry's, but she ignored it and carried on just as before.

The neighbour might have been worried, social services might have been on alert, but our mum wasn't bothered at all.

Chapter Six

By the time I turned eight and Tanya was eleven we looked like Barbie dolls. Our nails were painted, our faces were plastered with make-up and we wore mini-skirts, bras and tight, revealing tops.

Mum thought we looked great. She couldn't see a thing wrong with her daughters resembling two miniature hookers. She carried on encouraging Terry to buy us the kind of clothes and make-up that should have had an X-rating.

We were still going down to the social services offices every month, for our therapy session with the child and family team, which included Anna Smithson. She and the rest of the team had been expressing concerns for a while, but Mum just brushed them away and said that we loved our new look. And of course we did – we thought it was great to look so grown-up and to be allowed make-up. We thought it made us a bit special, and it felt nice to be special.

One day we turned up at social services and Anna failed to recognise Tanya at all. Her hair had been permed and she was wearing a push-up bra – despite the fact that she hadn't really got anything to be pushed up – a tight mini-skirt and high heels.

Anna looked grim, and asked Mum if she thought it was appropriate for Tanya to look like that. 'Yeah,' Mum grinned. 'She looks about eighteen, doesn't she? Not like other kids.'

'I think that's the problem,' Anna said quietly. 'An eleven-year-old should look her age.'

'Rubbish,' Mum sniffed. 'She looks great.'

Anna said nothing; she just looked worried as she carried on with our session, asking us how we all were. Tanya and I said what we always said – that we were fine and we liked Terry and everything was good. What else were we going to say? We knew that Mum would be livid if we gave away anything that spoiled her arrangement with Terry and took away her free goodies and convenient childcare. And besides, Terry now often came with us to the meetings. Every time he turned up with us Anna would say that the meeting was for family only, but Mum would just say that if Terry couldn't come too we were all leaving. Anna would be exasperated, but she had to give in or Mum would just march us all out. She called all the shots.

So Terry would sit and chat to Anna, just like one of the family, and we would all tell her that everything was fine. What else could we do?

But the truth was that everything was far from fine. Terry was still abusing both me and Tanya, whenever he could get Mum to let us stay the night. And Mum was only too willing, because it gave her the freedom to see her boyfriend and go out. She sent us over the road two or three times a week. And we went, without any objection. I hated what Terry did to us, and Tanya did too, but we knew it made Mum happy, and we did like the presents and treats we got at his house.

Jamie, who was ten, still came to the sessions, but he was becoming more and more reluctant and Mum was having trouble with him. Despite being so young, he was often violent and destructive, smashing things and lashing out at Mum, physically and verbally. He was excluded from school for scratching cars in the teachers' car park, and now he had started roaming the estate causing all kinds of trouble. He was regularly stealing car stereos, shoplifting and breaking into local houses to rob them. The police were often at our house, wanting to question him about yet another crime, but half the time Jamie had done a bunk and they couldn't find him.

He would sit sullenly through the sessions, refusing to talk to Anna and staring out of the window. And more often than not, Paul refused to come at all. He was fifteen and running wild. He did as he wanted and spent most of his time away from the house, seldom coming back, even at night. He had a gang of mates, but they weren't real friends. They bullied him and hit him and took his things and he put up with it because they were all he had.

By the time the Christmas holidays arrived, very little had changed. It was now over two years since George had gone to prison, and almost as long since we had met Terry. We had been handed from one abuser to the next, and despite all the attention we were getting from social services, no-one had worked out what was going on, or stepped in to stop it.

I was restless and bored in the holidays. Sometimes I played outside with some of the other kids on the estate, but I didn't have as many friends as Tanya did. I was less outgoing than I had been a couple of years earlier, my confidence had been crushed by all that had happened and I found it hard to talk to people. Tanya was so good at it – she was always more talkative and better at making friends than I was and she had a crowd of friends she hung out with. The boys were always out all day and I hadn't a clue where they were. Terry was at work, and Mum was usually to be found sitting in front of the TV, eating and drinking, or playing cards with Auntie Carol and Nanna. She wasn't interested in me – unless it was to order me to make them all butties or cups of tea. I used to get out of the house to avoid them all ordering me about and laughing at me, but then I'd find myself wandering around, scuffing my shoes and looking for someone to play with. I yearned for any bit of attention I could get.

I knew that Paul and his gang built dens and had secret hiding places. I was envious – I longed to be included, but they didn't even notice me. Then one day I saw Paul and several boys running out from an alleyway between two houses.

'Paul,' I shouted. 'What you doing? Can I play?'

He looked over at his mates. I expected them to burst out

laughing and shout 'No chance,' but to my surprise they beckoned me over. I ran after them, back up the alley. There were lots of empty houses on the estate back then, and Paul told me they had made a den in the back yard of one of them and I could come and see it.

Dead excited to be included, I grinned like a Cheshire cat.

'You've got to wear a blindfold,' Paul said. 'We can't have you telling everyone where our den is.'

'OK,' I said, nervous but determined to do whatever he said.

He took out a grubby scarf and tied it over my eyes, and then he and another boy, one each side, pushed me along the street, until we suddenly stopped.

'Here it is,' Paul said. 'But you can't look yet.'

'No,' another lad joined in, sneeringly. 'We need to make sure you won't remember where you've been.'

They started spinning me around and pushing me from one to the other. I began to feel sick and dizzy and scared.

'Paul, stop, I feel sick,' I said. But he laughed and then rough hands pulled my t-shirt up.

'Not much there, is there, lads,' one of them laughed, and they all started laughing and jeering.

Hot tears ran down my cheeks as I stood, dazed and confused.

'I don't understand,' I sobbed. 'Where's the den?'

'Stupid little idiot,' Paul spat. 'Do you honestly think we'd let you hang around with us? You're just good for a laugh, that's all.'

The boys ran off, laughing, leaving me to pull off the blindfold. I was standing in an empty house, with bare walls and some old cardboard on the floor. Still crying, I tried to straighten my clothes and wipe my eyes. They had just wanted to make a fool of me, they thought I was a joke. My brother had simply used me to amuse his mates.

I walked slowly out of the door into the street and looked round. I had no idea where I was. I set off up the street, looking for something I recognised, but it was another hour before I finally found my way home.

Later Paul came home and said to me, 'Not a word to Mum, do you understand? Or you'll be for it.' He looked so threatening that I just nodded silently.

A few days later, it happened all over again. Paul told me I really could see their den this time, he said they wanted to make up for frightening me. I went along with him, so desperate for attention that I didn't see what was coming. Once again I was blindfolded, taken to an empty house, and then shoved around and jeered at. They pushed me so hard that I fell over several times, and one of them tried to pull off my skirt. They carried on until they grew bored and ran off, leaving me to find my way home, sore, bruised and upset.

The whole thing was repeated several times over the next few weeks. Each time Paul said sorry and promised me sweets or a treat and, desperate to believe him, I went with him – only to find his mates waiting to shove me around and laugh at me.

I would go home and throw myself on my bed, crying into my pillow. Why was my own brother being so cruel to me? It just confirmed in my mind that I was boring and ugly and no-one wanted to be around me.

Then one day the police arrived at the door and said they were looking for Paul. Mum began shouting at them, asking what he'd done and telling them to get lost, but they ignored her and two policemen took Paul's arms and began marching him out towards their car.

Paul was crying and screaming at the top of his voice, pleading with Mum to help him. Seeing him in such a state, being dragged away from us, upset me dreadfully. I didn't have a clue what was happening or what it was about. All I knew was that he was crying for help and I couldn't help him.

Paul was taken into custody, along with several of his friends. It turned out that they had robbed a number of houses on the estate. They'd got away with it until someone lay in wait and caught them coming out of a house with their hands full of stolen goods.

Mum swore Paul didn't do anything wrong, and when he was found guilty and sent to a young offenders' unit, she was livid. She went round to the house where he'd been caught, banging on their door and yelling at the top of her voice, accusing them of lying.

Although it had been dreadful seeing Paul taken away, in some ways life without him was better – and not just because he wasn't tormenting me any more. Mum was much more relaxed and seemed less angry than normal, which made things easier for me, Tanya and Jamie. She had always saved the worst of her anger for Paul, and I used to wonder what it was about him that made her hate him so.

Her good mood evaporated, however, when we paid our next visit to see Anna at the social services offices. Mum stormed out of the room where Anna had taken her for a private chat, a furious look on her face. She grabbed us and headed home, without saying a word.

When we got back, Tanya whispered to me to come over to Terry's to get out of the way. But when she told Mum we were going over the road, Mum wouldn't let us. She said we weren't to go over there for a few days and he wasn't to come to our house, to 'keep them lot off our backs for a while' as she put it.

I was puzzled. Why would we need to stay away from Terry? None of us had said anything. What I didn't know then was that social services were suspicious about him and Anna had warned Mum to keep us away from him.

She lasted two days. After that things went back to normal. Terry came over to our house with a bag of goodies for Mum, and Tanya and I resumed our daily visits to his place.

The summer holidays had begun, and Mum announced she

was going away for a week with her boyfriend. She didn't mind taking Jamie, but she didn't want us girls so she asked Terry to have me and Tanya. He said he would take us on holiday, to see his parents in Bangor.

So two weeks after the warning from social services, Mum took off with Jamie, and Tanya and I set off on a coach with Terry, each of us carrying a small suitcase. We were excited to be going on a holiday. We'd only ever had a couple of holidays before, and they'd both been pretty awful. The first had been a few years earlier, when Mum and George took us to stay in a caravan by the sea. It wasn't much fun, because we had to do exactly as George said all the time, and that meant no running around and playing on the beach. There were a few photos of that holiday and they showed George – a massive man with hulking shoulders – next to four tiny kids, not one of us smiling. That said it all.

Our next holiday was after George went to prison, when social services sent us to a kids' camp for parents who were on benefits and couldn't afford holidays. The week before the holiday we had to have a medical. They recorded our height and weight and checked us for nits. When we got to the camp there was a pool – but not everyone could go in, you had to be chosen. The whole two weeks were regimented, just like the holiday with George. We ate, slept and played at set times. Wardens were in charge and if parents wrote to the children they opened the letters and took out any money. Mum didn't write, so we weren't bothered about that. But the wardens were unfriendly and shouted at us to get into line for everything and by the time we got home we were so glad that we didn't care if we never went on holiday again.

But the holiday with Terry would be different, we were sure of that. Tanya and I sat on the coach, chattering and looking out of the windows. We couldn't wait to catch our first glimpse of the sea.

Terry's parents lived in a small terraced house, a few streets from the sea front. They were both very old and didn't hear or see well. His dad had square black glasses with thick lenses and he smoked a pipe all day. His mum couldn't get about much, and hardly ever left the house. They both said hello, and then took very little notice of us after that. They must have wondered who exactly we were, and why their son had brought us, but they didn't say a word.

On the first day, Terry took us to the beach. It was wonderful and Tanya and I were wild with excitement. We spent the whole day splashing in the sea and building sandcastles together, while Terry sat and watched us.

Once again I was sleeping downstairs, on the couch, while Tanya was in a spare bedroom upstairs. And, as usual, Terry appeared in the night, once his parents were safely asleep. But this time, instead of forcing himself into my mouth or sticking his fingers and tongue into me, he got on top of me and tried to force his penis inside me. It hurt so much that instead of just lying there, as I usually did, I tried to push him away and pleaded with him to stop. He made a funny grunting noise, in frustration, and tried again and again. He refused to give up and in the end my small arms got too tired to push him away any longer.

I tried to switch off from the pain as Terry grunted on top of me. Why would someone who loved you do this? Why would they want to hurt you so much? I just couldn't understand it.

Every night of the holiday Terry tried to do the same thing. I tried to fight him off, and sometimes I won and he gave up. But more often he won, and I was left bruised and sore and in tears. By the end I was hurting inside and very sore and during the day I was finding blood in my knickers.

My struggles to push him away every night made him angry. Who was I to push him away, he would snarl. I felt helpless, but I couldn't block it out of my mind any more. The pain had become too much for me and, although I usually lost the battle, I continued to try to push him away.

It was the same with Tanya. I didn't know then that Terry was doing the same things to her, but as the week wore on she became quieter and there were dark circles under her eyes.

Over the course of that week Terry began to change. He became distant and angry. He sounded irritated every time he spoke to me, and he looked at me with a cold expression in his eyes. He wasn't nice to Tanya either, even though she had always been his favourite.

After that first outing to the beach, he refused to take us out again and we spent the rest of the holiday watching television and playing cards. The time dragged and it didn't feel much like a holiday at all.

I didn't like Terry any more. I couldn't wait to get home and away from him. If I had known the way, I would have walked all those miles back. As it was, I had to wait for the week to end, counting the days till I could get back home.

On the coach, Tanya and I both stared silently out of the window for the whole journey. When we got home, Mum was there, but she didn't bother asking about our week away, she just told us to keep it quiet if the social asked about our holiday. It turned out that social services had paid for a caravan for the four of us and Mum. She knew we would never have been allowed to go with Terry, but she didn't care. She lied to social services and used the caravan in Clacton for her holiday with John and Jamie.

I ran up to my bedroom and lay on my bed, clutching my teddy bear. Half an hour later I heard Jamie coming upstairs. He came into my room and started telling me what a great holiday he'd had in the caravan with Mum and John and how much fun they'd had. As he chattered on, I kept wondering why Mum didn't want to take me with her. My own mum would rather I go away with someone else for a holiday than take me with her. What was it that was so wrong with me? I felt sure I must be a really horrible person.

Jamie was telling me about the friends he'd made and the presents he'd had and all I could think about was what had happened to me on my holiday. I felt so sad and depressed and longed for someone to give me a hug and show me they cared. I must have had a distant look in my eyes, because Jamie suddenly stopped and said, 'What's up with you?'

I wondered whether I could tell him. I wanted to, so much. Perhaps Jamie would understand, and help me to feel better.

'I've got tummy ache down there,' I said hesitantly, pointing between my legs. 'It really hurts and it's been bleeding. It's all in my knickers.'

'What've you done, fallen over or something?' Jamie said.

'No,' I said quietly, my voice wobbling. 'It's Terry. He's been doing rude things to me, touching me . . . down there.'

Jamie burst out laughing. 'Who'd wanna touch you?' he scoffed. Then he told me not to be stupid and that Mum would be angry if she heard me saying those things, before heading out of the door, back to his own room.

I sat on my bed, tears rolling down my cheeks. That was it. I'd tried to tell someone, and he had just laughed. Why did I expect anything else? No-one was going to believe me. And, in any case, it was my fault it had happened. I was a bad girl and I made all these people do nasty things to me. I lay back on the bed. My body ached and I felt all the energy drain from me. I grabbed hold of my quilt cover and pulled it up towards my face to wipe my tears.

I must have fallen asleep. I woke to hear Mum shouting up the stairs that tea was ready. Slowly, I got to my feet and made my way down. When I got there, Mum and Jamie were already sitting on the sofa, tucking into their food, the television blaring in front of them.

'It's in the kitchen,' Mum called, without taking her eyes from the television. Tanya walked out of the kitchen holding two plates and passed me one as she sat down. I could tell Tanya wasn't her normal self either, but at that stage I didn't realise that Terry had been doing the same things to her and she was also traumatised.

Jamie was still banging on about his holiday. He seemed to be enjoying the fact that Tanya and I looked miserable. I kept quiet – I had already been humiliated once and I wasn't going to risk it again – but Tanya suddenly spoke.

'Mum,' she said. Mum, engrossed in her programme, didn't appear to hear her.

'Mum,' she tried again. 'Terry tried it on with me.'

I stared hard at my plate, trying to see sideways what Mum's reaction was. She carried on eating, and for a minute we thought she hadn't heard. Then she said, 'So what did he do to you?'

Tanya took a breath. 'He tried kissing me and touching me, but I kept pushing him off and hitting him.'

'Well, as long as he knows then,' Mum replied. I had expected fireworks and a blazing row, but Mum could have been discussing a shopping list for all the emotion she showed.

I looked up at Tanya. Her face looked tired, her expression almost blank. I could see the emptiness in her eyes, and the hopelessness she felt. I realised then that she had been through the same ordeal as me. We had both tried to push Terry off, and we had both failed.

Neither of us said another word, and Mum didn't mention it again. We finished our tea and cleared the plates and I went back to the living room and sat down, staring at the clock, wishing the day would end. But it wasn't just the day I wanted to end, it was my life. I felt numb. There didn't seem any point in going on. People who said they loved me kept hurting me and no-one wanted to listen or help. I was sore and tired and sad and hurt, and it felt as though nothing was ever going to make it better. I was nine years old and my life didn't seem worth living.

Chapter Seven

The following morning, Tanya and I got up and got ourselves ready for school. Neither of us said anything about what had happened with Terry or Mum's reaction. There seemed to be an unwritten rule that we should never talk about it. We both knew that Terry had done the same frightening, painful things to both of us. We didn't need to say anything; it was as though we could read each other's minds. A look was enough to tell us that we knew and understood and shared the hurt. Tanya and I were the same: children trapped in a world we didn't understand, crying out for love and attention, betrayed and let down by the people who should have loved and protected us.

That morning we were like wounded creatures, limping along, trying to find a way to pick up the pieces of our lonely existence and carry on. Tanya, so often the chatty one, was unusually quiet. She hardly said a word all the way to school. I didn't know it then, but it had all got too much for her, she couldn't hold in the pain any longer. Later that day, she broke down in tears at school and told her teacher everything.

In the afternoon, I was called out of class and taken into

an office where one of the teachers was sitting with the head teacher. She told me not to worry or be frightened, but that Tanya had said some things about Terry. She asked me if anything had happened to me when I was with him. She was kind, her voice was soft and she held my hand, and that was all I needed. I began to cry, and to tell her what Terry had done and how much it had hurt and how scared I'd been. She stayed calm and quiet, and I was so glad there was no shouting. It was a relief to get it all out. After I had finished, she thanked me for telling her and said I was to go back to my class. I felt shaky and a bit worried about whether I'd been right to tell, but I didn't dare ask her what would happen now.

Tanya and I walked home together, both of us quiet, neither of us mentioning what had happened. I'm sure we were both thinking the same thing – please don't let Mum find out that we told.

At home everything seemed normal. We had our tea in front of the TV, relieved that everything seemed OK. But before we'd finished we heard a commotion going on outside. Jamie went to the window and shouted, 'It's the police; they're outside Terry's house.' Mum shot across to the window, and Tanya and I followed her. We didn't look at one another.

The image of Terry being taken away by the police is one I will never forget. I stared, transfixed, as he was brought out of his house, a policeman holding each arm. He looked up and his eyes didn't move from the window where we stood.

I wanted to run and hide but I couldn't move; I was stuck to the spot, horrified.

Mum's reaction was extraordinary. She must have been told what Tanya and I had said – social services would have informed her – but she didn't let on. Instead, she started laughing out loud. Grinning from ear to ear, she opened the window and shouted, 'You're not laughing now, are you?' as he was pushed into the back of the police car. It was as though she was enjoying the show. She seemed amused by the fact that Terry was no longer in control, and behaved as if she had been calling the shots all along. She didn't appear angry that her daughters had been abused, or to blame herself for encouraging him to become part of our family and have me and Tanya over at his house. To see her then, you would think it was all a big laugh.

I didn't know what to think. I was unnerved by the way Terry had stared at us. I felt his eyes had been fixed on me alone, and was terrified he would find a way to get revenge on me. But even worse than that was my fear about what would happen next. What had we done? What would Mum do? What would happen to us? The anxiety paralysed me, as I watched the police car drive away with Terry in the back.

As soon as it was out of sight, Mum turned to me and Tanya. 'What were you playing at? Both of you are old enough to look after yourselves and look what you've done now,' she yelled. 'You should have said no; you know it's wrong,' she spat. 'God knows what they'll do now.' Tanya and I stood silent under her onslaught, heads bowed, as she cursed us again and then grabbed her cup of coffee and walked off.

That evening, she sat in front of the TV, drinking one cup of coffee after another, as Tanya and I crept around the house, both of us miserable and wishing we'd never said anything. Jamie, mirroring Mum's reaction, told us he didn't believe us. He said we were lying to get Terry into trouble and that he was ashamed to have two sisters like us.

The next morning, Anna from social services arrived, with another woman, and drove Mum, Tanya and me to the social services offices, where we sat in a waiting room with another social worker. Then Tanya and I were taken, one at a time, into an office where two more people were sitting behind a desk. When it was my turn, they asked me lots of questions about Terry and his friendship with our family and what he had done. I told them everything I could remember, but all the time I was feeling scared and worried that we shouldn't have said anything. First George and now Terry. Mum was very angry and upset and it was our fault.

Over the next couple of weeks, things got even worse. In police interviews, Terry denied touching us, so Tanya and I were subjected to endless interviews, medicals and examinations. It was far worse than it had been after George. We were taken to all kinds of different places, where different people asked us to tell them all over again what had happened. We were told by the people who interviewed us that it wasn't our fault and we weren't to blame, but we didn't believe that for one minute.

The medical examinations were the worst. They hurt dreadfully, and this time they took photos of me with no clothes on and my legs apart. I felt so upset I just closed my eyes and tried to count, like I did when George and Terry were doing what they did to me. It didn't feel any different.

It turned out that I'd suffered an internal tear to the vagina wall, which was why I had bled so much. It had healed by this time, but there was a scar. And both Tanya and I had chlamydia, a sexually transmitted infection that we needed pills and creams for.

We got home after the medicals and interviews feeling tired and confused and emotionally wrung out. We needed to be held and comforted and reassured that no-one would hurt us again. Instead, Mum started on us, blaming us for ruining her life. She was angry all the time, and either ignored us or told us we'd caused her trouble she didn't need. 'Why couldn't you have just told him no, instead of getting social services and the police on our backs,' she'd yell.

She behaved as though it was she who had been the victim. Her new relationship was coming to an end under all the pressure, and she paced around the house, drinking, smoking and shouting at us.

To make things even worse, some of the neighbours abused

us on a daily basis, smashing our front windows and yelling from outside the house, calling me and Tanya slags. Why they turned on two children, I don't really know, except that they hated Mum and somehow that rubbed off on all of us. One of them had called social services in the first place, but it wasn't out of concern for us kids, it was to get at Mum. We would watch Mum chasing people down the street with a hammer or anything else she could lay her hands on, screaming and swearing and calling them interfering bastards and telling them to keep their noses out.

Then came the day when I was called out of class and told I had to go home. I got there to find Tanya and Jamie had been called home too. Mum was in her bedroom, crying her eyes out. She said she couldn't go on, and that she was going to end everything. We begged her not to, and when she said she wanted John, Jamie ran round to his house to get him. He came over, and sat with Mum and calmed her down. But once again we were left feeling that we had made her want to die. We couldn't have understood then that it was probably all just a ploy to hang onto John.

Our life was quickly falling apart at the seams. But worse was to come. The next few days were the most dreadful time I had ever lived through. For all her faults, I could never have imagined being anywhere else but with Mum. She was a terrible parent who had no idea of the difference between right and wrong, and no idea how to protect her children, but in her own warped way I think she loved us. Certainly we loved her. Throughout all the awfulness we had been through, Mum had been there, even if she didn't really have any idea how to care for us and let us down on a daily basis. I had no idea that we were going to lose her too, until one wet spring day shortly after Terry was arrested.

And despite all I had been through in my nine short years, that has stayed in my memory as the most horrendous time of all.

It was about two weeks after Terry had gone, and life was just beginning to get back to normal. School had finished and Tanya and I had made our way home through the back alley and onto our street. That's when we spotted the police cars in front of our house. We weren't too worried at first – they'd been back a few times since they'd taken Terry, because of the disturbances between Mum and the neighbours

But as we got nearer I knew something wasn't right. Nanna was there with her arm around Mum, who was crying and shouting. There must have been five or six other people gathered in the front garden: a couple of police officers and a few others we didn't know. Then I saw that Jamie was there, and a strange man was standing next to him with his arm around his shoulders.

Tanya began to run towards them and, suddenly feeling very scared, I followed, chasing her and yelling at her to wait for me. But she was too fast. She tore up the street and into the garden, where she headed towards Mum, who by this time was becoming completely hysterical. But before Tanya could reach her, a lady I didn't know and a policewoman grabbed hold of her and held her back.

When I got there I stopped at the bottom of the path, confused and frightened and unsure what to do. Then I saw Anna Smithson. She smiled at me, but she looked uncomfortable and I could tell she was hiding something.

Mum was still shouting, but I couldn't make out what she was saying, only our names, which she called out again and again. I ran towards her, but Anna stepped forward and stopped me.

I burst into tears. I didn't know what was going on, but I was sure it was something very bad. 'What's happening, Mum?' I screamed. Tanya, Jamie and I were all being held back by the people in the garden and we were looking at Mum, desperate for her to tell us what it was all about, but she just continued to cry and scream.

Anna leaned down towards my ear and spoke gently. 'Come on, Louise, it's time to go, sweetheart.'

Go? Go where? What was she talking about? I was becoming frantic.

'Mum,' I called, pulling away from Anna. 'What's happening? Mum, please.'

'They're taking you away from me, they're taking you all away from me,' she shouted, her voice breaking.

At that moment my heart seemed to explode, sending shock

waves through my small body. I started to tremble violently and to sob so hard my throat hurt. What had we done? Why were we being taken away?

It seemed as though we were being punished twice – once by Terry and now by the social services, who had decided to take us away from our mum. Years later I was able to understand that they felt it was in our best interests. But the way they did it was brutal and insensitive. And what they didn't know, because they had never asked me, was that I could take all the beatings, all the sexual abuse, all the loneliness and neglect, the daily put downs and the lack of love and affection, but I couldn't bear being taken away from Mum. This was my home and my family and all I had ever known. Nothing could have prepared me for that moment, when I realised I was going to lose them. I felt as if I had been cut open and my insides were spilling out on the floor.

I looked around, searching for answers that weren't there, staring at the strangers who were taking us. I looked over at Jamie, hoping he could do something, but he looked as scared as I felt.

Anna tried again. 'Louise, come on, let's go.'

'No . . . no . . . no,' I yelled.

I felt sure we were being sent to the same place that Paul had gone to, as a punishment for what we had done. I had no idea we were being taken for our own protection. I was convinced we were going to jail.

'I'm sorry, I'm sorry,' I sobbed. How I wished we had kept quiet and not said anything.

Anna had hold of my arm. I struggled to pull away from her, then another lady grabbed hold of my other arm and between them they pulled and shoved me into the back of the police car. Tanya and Jamie were calmer and walked to the car on their own. Perhaps they understood more about what was going on, or perhaps they just realised there was no point in fighting.

Sitting beside me in the back seat, Jamie did something he had never done before. He put his arms round me and told me not to cry and that it would be OK.

But it wasn't OK. My throat ached from screaming and tears poured down my face. It wasn't OK and it wasn't going to be OK.

Through the car window, I could see Mum trying desperately to fight her way over to us. There were several police officers holding her back. Then the car was moving and we were off down the street, with me still sobbing and Jamie and Tanya sitting quietly either side of me, staring at the floor.

It's hard to describe how I felt at that moment. I knew that my life would never be the same again, ever. I had lost my mum and my home and I was being taken somewhere I didn't want to go and there was nothing I could do to stop it. I felt as if my world was ending. I was being punished for telling on George and Terry. Mum was all I had, I loved her, and now even she was gone.

The drive seemed to last a lifetime. Anna was in the front of the car, beside the policeman who was driving, and she explained, twisting in her seat to look at us, that we were going to a nice place where we would all be safer. I didn't understand at all. What did she mean we would be much safer where we were going? They had taken us away from our mum – how were we going to feel safer?

A while later, we pulled up outside a large red-brick building with big windows. It looked really old, like a haunted house in a film. Anna led us up the steps. 'This is a children's home,' she told us. 'I'm sure you'll like it here.'

When we reached the front door, a lady opened it and said hello, before leading us into a large entrance hall. Anna came in with us, and then said goodbye and told us that we'd be looked after here and that she'd come and see us tomorrow.

Our feet echoed on the bare wooden floor as we were ushered into a small office with white walls and a table and several chairs in the middle of it. To one side were a desk and a few filing cabinets, with boxes piled up next to them. As we stood in the doorway, a woman got up from behind the desk and came towards us. 'Hello,' she said. 'My name is Ruth and I'm in charge here. Come and sit down.'

Silently, we filed in and sat in the chairs around the table, all three of us white-faced with shock. I had cried so much I felt completely drained and exhausted. My body ached and my eyes looked dully around without really seeing. I didn't care what they said to us or what they did. I just wanted to go home to Mum.

Ruth spoke for the next few minutes, but I don't think any of us took in a word she said. She sounded calm, but brisk and not very friendly. I looked over at Tanya, hoping that she would be able to make some sense out of all this and explain what was going on, but she looked empty and sad and blank. It was as though we all felt this wasn't really happening at all and we were in the middle of a bad dream.

Sadly, though, it was no dream. This big, ugly, cold house was to be our home now. That much I understood.

When Ruth had finished talking, a lady came in with a plate of sandwiches. We'd missed tea, Ruth said, so this was all they could do. The three of us sat over our plates without saying a word. I didn't even see the sandwiches in front of me. I put one in my mouth and it tasted like cardboard. I felt as if I was going to be sick.

After tea, Ruth took us to see the rooms where we would be sleeping. The first door she opened was at the top of the stairs. 'This is where you'll be, Louise,' she said. I stared at the little room, with its single bed, and my lips wobbled as it dawned on me that I was to be in here on my own. For the first time in my life, Tanya wasn't going to be with me. I felt panicky and my eyes filled with tears. Where would Tanya be? And what if I needed her or got scared in the night? I wouldn't even be able to leave the door open; all the rooms had heavy fire-doors which slammed shut behind you. I wanted to beg Ruth to let me sleep with Tanya, but I didn't dare say a word.

Tanya and Jamie were shown to identical rooms further along the corridor. Then we were taken back downstairs into what Ruth called the games room. It was a big, open-plan room with a dining table and a hatch through to the kitchen at one end, and a pool table, a TV and some arcade machines at the other end. Eight or nine rough-looking kids – all of them older than me and Tanya – were playing pool or standing around the arcade machines.

The three of us hung back, awkward and shy, as the kids sized us up. None of them spoke to us, and we didn't join in, we just went over to some seats near the TV and sat there, staring at it without even noticing what was on.

That evening, Nanna came over with some of our things in a small suitcase. We were allowed to talk to her for a few minutes. I was glad to see Nanna, who was a little warmer than usual. She asked if we were all right and told us Mum was crying, so she couldn't stay long, as she needed to get back to her. She told us Mum wouldn't be allowed to come and see us for a while, and I started crying again. Nanna said she would come back and see us again soon, then she left.

That night I unpacked the little suitcase. Only my clothes

were in it. Not my teddy or my beloved doll. I got into the cold bed and lay there, feeling more alone than ever before. I had cried so much I had no more tears; I just stared into the darkness, wishing I had my little doll, Amber, to cuddle, or the comforting sound of Tanya's breathing on the other side of the room.

I had lost everything. Now I had to live in this ugly house, where I didn't want to be, with new people who were nothing to do with me. The only thing that hadn't changed was the way I felt. Unloved, uncared for and lost.

Chapter Eight

In the end I must have slept a little. I woke when Ruth came in and told me to get dressed and come down for breakfast. I felt heavy and tired, but I dragged myself up, put on my clothes and went down to the dining area. When I got there, most of the other kids were already sitting around the big table.

There were about ten of us altogether. I was the youngest – most of the rest were teenagers who ignored me or looked at me as if I was something the cat had brought in. I sat down and looked around for the food. Then I realised that none of the kids were eating – they seemed to be waiting for something. A couple of minutes later, a boy of about fifteen sauntered in. He went over to the counter where the cereals were laid out and helped himself, before coming over to sit down. After that, everyone else went to get some cereal.

I didn't understand it, but I soon learned that the boy was called Wayne and he was king pin. He'd been there longer than anyone else, which seemed to give him the right to do as he chose. If you didn't give him first pick of all the meals, he would get you alone later and give you a beating. The staff knew this, but they took no notice and just let him do it.

I was shocked. It made me hate the place even more than I already did. It certainly wasn't at all like a real home. It was cold and unfriendly and the staff didn't seem interested in the children – it was clearly just a job to them. Ruth, the one we'd already met, was the manager. She was in her thirties, short and chunky, and, as we discovered, she only ever dressed in the same clothes – a t-shirt, jumper and jeans. She spent a lot of time in the kitchen or in her office, drinking endless cups of black coffee. She wasn't the sort of person you could approach with a problem or a worry; she just didn't want to be bothered by the kids. Another staff member, Nathan, was in his thirties. He was very quiet and paced around with his hands behind his back. We thought he was a bit weird. There were several others who did shifts and then disappeared, but Ruth seemed to be there the whole time.

For the first couple of weeks, I found it very difficult to settle, especially at night. My small bedroom had heavy cord carpet on the floor and a bed like the ones in hospital. Nothing about it was friendly or warm, and when I went to bed, even though I was tired, I didn't want to close my eyes. It was all too scary and different and horrible. I knew Tanya and Jamie were in rooms down the corridor and I wished I could see them, but I didn't dare get up and go and look for them.

Early on, Ruth came in and went through all my clothes, taking away the more precocious ones that Terry had bought. I didn't understand why at the time, and felt angry that not even my clothes were mine any more. Strangely, I was still allowed to wear make-up; the staff didn't seem to mind. No doubt they had their own reasons for letting me carry on, but whatever they were, I was delighted, and used to put on as much make-up as I could whenever I wasn't at school.

During our first few days, Tanya and I were taken to visit the local primary school, where we would be starting. I didn't care what it looked like, it was just another school. I wanted my old school, where at least everything was familiar. After the visit, we went to get our uniforms – navy blue skirts, ties and jumpers, with white shirts. This cheered me a little. I loved having a uniform instead of tatty old clothes – for the first time I would be the same as the other kids in school.

Jamie was allowed to stay at his old school, and was sent there by taxi, while Nathan walked me and Tanya to our new school the day after we got our uniforms. It was only ten minutes away, and after that, he said, we would be walking there on our own.

The teacher, who was tall and slim with long blonde hair, introduced me to the class. She was nice, but I felt lost. It was halfway through the term and I had no idea how to fit in or what to do. At breaktimes I wandered around, trying to find someone to talk to, but most of the kids ignored me. The only person who spoke to me was a boy with bright orange hair. He said his name was Mark, and he was nice. He was to be my only real friend while I was there – the two of us were outcasts together – and although we weren't very close, it meant I had someone to talk to.

I never told any of the kids that I was in care. I already felt different from the rest of them, without that to complicate things even further.

I struggled with the work, as I was miles behind everyone else. There was no extra help; I was just expected to manage. I did my best, but it was impossible for me to catch up, so I always felt like the stupid one.

After the first few weeks, I did manage to get talking to a girl called Poppy – someone else who didn't really have any friends – and I was thrilled when she asked me to tea. I skipped the whole way home that day, wondering what her house would be like and what we would have to eat. But my hopes were dashed when I rushed in to ask Ruth if I could go and she told me that everyone in Poppy's family would have to be police-checked before I could visit their house. I was sure they would never agree, so it was with a heavy heart and deep embarrassment that I went to school the next day and told Poppy the news – begging her not to tell the other kids that I was in care.

I never did get to go to her house. From then on, Poppy began to give me a wide berth. No doubt she'd been warned to stay away from me because her parents didn't want her hanging around with a girl from a kids' home, especially one with a reputation for housing out-of-control kids who went around the neighbourhood spraying graffiti, smashing swings in the playground at the park and drinking and smoking.

After that, I didn't really try to be friends with anyone. I just hung around by myself. I told myself I didn't care – I'd never had any friends before, so why should it be different now? People had always thought I was trash. But deep down it hurt me badly, knowing that now I was in a children's home my last hope of being able to make a friend was gone.

At Cranley it was the kids who were in charge, not the adults. It was more like a youth club with bedrooms than a real home. Top of the roost was Wayne, who terrorised everyone, even the staff. They would turn a blind eye as he battered and bullied any kid who stood in his way. Wayne had first pick of everything – from the clothes and food to what we watched on TV that night. It was more like a prison, where the toughest inmates ruled, than a home for children.

Jamie fell out with him several times. He couldn't see why Wayne should have his pick of everything, so he refused to put up with it, and Wayne was furious. He hit Jamie many times, making his nose bleed and on one occasion getting him on the floor and kicking him. The staff saw what was going on, but they didn't intervene.

The boys in the home were constantly fighting. There were punch-ups every day. Most of them were ignored by the staff, but one night there was such a massive brawl that the staff had to jump in and break it up before several boys got badly hurt. As ever, Wayne was at the centre of it.

Jamie, Tanya and I quickly realised that to survive we were going to have to toughen up. If we wanted to avoid becoming targets for bullying, we had to join in with being rude to the staff, swearing all the time and taking the mickey out of anyone who was ripe for picking on. Not surprisingly, our behaviour deteriorated fast. Desperate to impress the older, tougher kids, I went from being quiet and shy to becoming a disruptive, argumentative kid, looking out for trouble with anyone who got in my way.

I also started smoking. All the kids used to go out and smoke in the garden after tea and, determined to be one of the gang, I asked them for a cigarette. They laughed and gave me one, and I tried hard to smoke it. But the smoke burned my throat, my face turned red and I struggled not to choke. I got through a third of it before I handed it to someone else. But after that I tried again and again, until, well before my tenth birthday, I could inhale with the best of them.

Most of the older kids hardly ever went to school, and Tanya and I soon began bunking off to hang out with them. I didn't mind school, but I wanted to be one of the gang, so a couple of times a week I followed Tanya to the park where we met up with the older ones, who'd bunked off too. We would go to the town centre, where there were shops to wander around. No-one seemed to notice that we weren't in school in the middle of the day.

There weren't many rules in the home. Most of the older kids were allowed to come and go as they pleased, but, to my frustration, I wasn't allowed out unsupervised. All I could do was go for a walk with a staff member, to the local shops or the park – and that would end when the staff member got fed-up and announced we were going back.

At weekends I became incredibly bored and the days dragged. We were allowed to lie in until nine or ten and very little was organised for us to do. We would play up all the time, chasing each other around, screaming and shouting, letting off fire extinguishers and smashing things up. We were never allowed to eat or drink except at set meal times. The kitchen was kept locked and the fridge and food cupboards had big bolts on them, to keep us all out.

To an outsider looking in, we would have looked like a bunch of out-of-control kids who didn't know how to behave. But we had all been so badly let down – by our families and then again by the care system, which allowed us to run riot, without providing stability, discipline, activities, or carers who actually cared. We were all just desperate for love and attention, and the only way we knew how to get attention was by misbehaving.

Anna came to see us regularly. She was always warm and concerned. She would ask how things were, and I'd tell her they were OK. I wasn't able to articulate my worries and fears, but it was nice to have someone who cared. I liked Anna, and looked forward to her visits.

I missed Mum badly and longed for her to come and see us. Tanya and I kept asking the staff if she could come, but the answer was always 'not yet'. We were allowed to ring her sometimes, but it was always awkward, as we didn't really know what to say. Mum was cheerful and I got the feeling that she was getting on fine without us and didn't really miss us or want us back.

We had been there for three months when we were told that Mum would be coming for an hour-long supervised visit.

A room in the home was laid aside for visits – a really nice room which didn't fit in with the rest of the place. It was bright and colourful, with comfy chairs, nice-looking and welcoming. One of the workers at the home would be supervising the visit, which meant she would sit in the corner of the room watching us for the whole time Mum was there.

The first time Mum came, all three of us were waiting for her in the visiting room. I felt excited and nervous, wondering how she was and if she was going to tell us that we could go home. I still didn't really know why we had been taken away from her. I wanted someone to explain, but I didn't dare ask.

When Mum finally arrived, Tanya and I rushed forward to hug her, with Jamie following behind. We were so happy to see her, and Mum seemed happy to see us too. She had brought sweets and presents and it really felt as though she missed and loved us. For the first time in our lives, she held us and cuddled us, touched us gently and stroked our faces. I lapped it up, wanting to hold onto Mum for the whole hour, drinking in the feeling of being loved.

All too soon, the hour was up and Mum had to go. The care worker stood up and said it was time, and I burst into tears, wanting Mum to stay, or to be allowed to go home with her. But the rule was strict and Mum was whisked out, promising she would come back when the next visit was allowed, in a fortnight.

Two whole weeks before we could spend another hour with her. It seemed such a long time. To me it was just as if we were in prison. After all, what was the difference? We were locked away, and had to wait for visiting time once a fortnight, when our every move would be watched.

Mum was always on her best behaviour. She really did seem to want to see us, and to have us back. She told us she hoped that we would eventually be allowed home. She said she didn't know why we had been taken away from her, and that we should nag the staff to let us see her, so that they would send us home. When she said that, I felt happy – it seemed as if she did really want us back. And after a few months of the fortnightly visits she was allowed to step them up to once – and sometimes even twice – a week. She was also allowed to see us unsupervised, though still only for an hour. I loved those visits, because Mum was still being really nice to us, even without the carer watching.

But it was at one of these meetings that she dropped a bombshell. Casually, as if she was discussing the weather, she told us that she had decided to move John and his two children in with her. She said she was lonely and needed the company now we had left her. My heart sank. We knew she was still seeing John, but now it felt as if we had been replaced just as easily as we had been taken away.

I didn't speak at all, and Mum must have sensed my unease. She tried to convince me that it was for the best and that we would all be together when we were allowed back home. I forced a smile but deep down I was hurting dreadfully. How could she just go and find other children to replace us? I felt rejected and unwanted, and nothing Mum or anyone else said made me feel any better. I felt we had just been thrown out, like pieces of rubbish.

After that, my behaviour rapidly went further downhill. I felt I had nothing more to lose, and I was badly behaved, angry and disruptive. No-one could get through to me – not that they really tried – and I didn't care if I was punished.

Shortly after this, Tanya, Jamie and I were given news that devastated us all over again. Ruth took us into her office and explained that we were to be moved to another home – one we would be settled in long-term.

The last thing I wanted was to move again. While I had hated the home at the start, after seven months I had got used to it and found a way to cope. I knew my way around, was settling in at school, and had learned to live with it. I thought we would be there until we went home, and I believed we'd be going home any day. Now there would be yet another place to get used to, more kids to get to know, and – worst of all – another school.

Ruth explained that it wasn't safe for the three of us to go back home yet. We just didn't get this at all. How come Mum could live with other kids, but not us? The stuffing was well and truly knocked out of all three of us. It felt so unfair, and no matter how Ruth put things, it didn't feel any better. To us it was just another kick in the teeth from adults who pretended they cared about us, but didn't really.

No-one ever reassured us, or explained that it was because we had been hurt and that they wanted to look after us. I think if they had, it would have helped. We'd still have been away from home, but we'd have understood that we weren't being punished. As it was, I didn't see that at all. I thought I must be the worst child in the world, unwanted, unloved and banned from my own home. I was convinced it was all a punishment for telling about George and Terry.

I think Tanya felt the same way. She barely spoke for the rest of the evening. I wished we could comfort one another, but neither of us knew how, so we just got on with what we had to do. As for Jamie, he just went out and kicked a football around, which was his way of venting his feelings.

What could we do? With tight, white faces, the three of us went reluctantly to our rooms to pack. We were due to leave the next morning. I asked if I could go to school to say goodbye to my teacher, and Ruth agreed. Nathan walked me to the local shop so that I could buy a big bar of Galaxy with my pocket money and then we walked to school.

I wasn't wearing my uniform, and the whole class watched in silence as I went in and gave the chocolate to the teacher. She didn't seem surprised, so she must have been told that I was going. I said goodbye and started to cry, and Nathan led me out and back to the home.

Later that day, Mum arrived for a visit. She walked in and told us she had brought John and his children, to introduce them to us. Her timing couldn't have been worse. We went out to the car park, where they were all standing around John's car, and I looked at the two children and thought, 'This is who Mum's got in to replace us.' They were just ordinary kids, and I knew it wasn't their fault, but I hated them all the same.

Tanya, Jamie and I stared sullenly as Mum told us they were called Shaun and Kelly. Then, after a couple more awkward minutes, they all got in the car and drove off, waving at us as they left.

Chapter Nine

Ten minutes after Mum left with her new family, Anna arrived to collect me, Jamie and Tanya. We were told to get into the back of her car and were taken right across the city, to an area we'd never heard of.

On the journey, Anna told us how lovely our new home was, and that there would be lots of people we could make friends with and a really nice school. But we stared out of the windows and said nothing. We didn't believe a word of it. I had always liked Anna, but at that moment I hated her. I was angry with her for stopping us going home with Mum – as far as I was concerned, it was all her fault, and a bit of sweet-talking wasn't about to win me over.

A short while later, we drew up outside a new-looking building with lots of flowers in the front garden. It was long and L-shaped, a kind of bungalow, with an upper floor that looked like a loft conversion, with a sloping roof. It was bright and clean and looked a lot nicer than the last home, but I was in no mood to care.

We walked from the small car park up the front path to the front door. Inside, a very short woman with spiky blonde hair

greeted us. I couldn't help staring at her, and as Anna introduced me, Jamie and Tanya, the lady winked at me. Despite
my glum mood, I giggled, and this made Tanya smile and
broke the ice. The lady told us her name was Penny and she
was in charge of the house. She thanked Anna for bringing
us and Anna gave us a quick hug, wished us luck and said
she'd see us in a couple of days.

I had to admit that the place looked nice. It was light and
airy and was decorated in peaches and creams, with soft carpet
on the floor and plants on the window sills. The atmosphere
seemed a lot calmer and more settled than it had been at
Cranley.

Penny took us into her office, which had kids' paintings all
over the wall, and gave us some tea and biscuits. She told us
this place was called Cherry Road and was home to around
twelve children. She said they took boys and girls from the
ages of eight to sixteen, though as there were no younger
ones at the moment, I would be the youngest.

'I hope you'll be happy here,' she smiled. 'Shall I show you
your rooms?'

We went upstairs to the corridor where the bedrooms were.
To my surprise and relief, Tanya and I were sharing again –
a small but pretty room with a sloping roof and skylight
windows that made it feel really cosy. Jamie was in a room
just down the hall, sharing with a boy called Ian.

Back downstairs, Penny introduced us to two of the other

staff members – Melanie and Craig. Later we met Ted and Janice, when they came on shift. All of them were nice, friendly, interested and kind. I was bowled over by how different they were to the staff at the previous home, but I wasn't about to show it. I still felt too hurt and upset to show any positive feelings, even though I was secretly surprised by how nice everything at Cherry Road was.

We met the other kids when they got back from school that day. Most of them were teenagers, and there were more girls than there had been at our last place. They didn't fall over themselves to be friendly, but they weren't hostile either. One of them, Monica, was seventeen and she had a baby. She lived in a little self-contained apartment at the end of the main building and she told us her boyfriend was allowed to visit her there. Her fifteen-year-old sister, Lizzie, was in Cherry Road too.

That night we were given spaghetti bolognese for tea. I'd never heard of it, but it was delicious – loads better than the boring food we'd had at the last place. I ate with gusto.

While things were much more pleasant at Cherry Road, the rules were far stricter. Penny was friendly but very firm and everyone had to do as they were told or face trouble. My bedtime was to be at nine every night – nine thirty at weekends – and no argument. We all had to help with the chores – a rota for washing-up, sweeping, setting tables and so on would be put up every week – and bad behaviour wasn't tolerated. If you stepped out of line, the punishment would be doing all the washing-up for a fortnight, or loss of TV privileges or pocket money.

But while the staff were tough about the rules, they were also much more involved and interested in the children. They were always about, and ready to have a chat or join in a game.

In this gentler, safer and more supportive environment I would gradually begin to find some healing. But it was to be a long process. I was a damaged, frightened, lonely child, and I didn't trust anyone. I had learned to lash out at anyone who came near me, and to keep myself to myself. I felt betrayed and let down by everyone. I'm sure I presented the staff with a huge challenge, but they weren't about to give up on me, and in time I realised it.

One day they asked me to fill in a form that asked 'What do you want in life?' I wrote that I just wanted to go home, have long hair, get a Barbie and go to Disneyland. I may have been wearing make-up and trying to compete with the teenagers, but in reality I was still just a small girl who wanted the things most other small girls want.

We were already into the autumn term when we arrived there. Penny told me I would be going to St Mark's Primary School, a ten-minute walk away. A couple of days after we arrived, Janice walked me into town to get my uniform. This time it was a grey skirt with a white shirt and red jumper and tie. I liked it, but I pretended I didn't.

A few days later, I started school. Janice walked me there and took me in. It was an old Victorian building, a little like my first school back at home. To me it was just another school, with yet another teacher and another set of kids. They eyed me curiously when I was taken in, and at breaktime a few of them tried to talk to me, but I was too shy and over-whelmed to respond, and after a while they gave up.

The school wasn't bad. Mostly no-one bullied me and I didn't mind being there, though I was still very behind and struggled with lessons, especially anything involving writing. I bunked off a few times at first, because that's what I was used to doing. I did a bit of shoplifting – nicking sweets and drinks. But apart from that, there wasn't really anything to do, so after I'd spent a few days walking around, thoroughly bored, I decided I might as well go to school.

I used to watch the most popular girl, who was always surrounded by friends. She was called Karen, and she reminded me of Amber Smith. Just as I had with Amber, back at my first school, I wondered what it would be like to be so pretty and popular.

One Saturday I was in our bedroom when Tanya came in and said, 'Karen's come to call for you.' I shot out of the door, wild with excitement. At last someone wanted to play with me, and not just someone, one of the most popular girls in the school. I raced to the front door, only to find there was no-one there. I turned to see Tanya laughing at me. 'Idiot,' she said. 'Did you really think she would want to play with you?' I was broken-hearted.

That wasn't the only time Tanya played that trick on me. I fell for it two or three more times. I was really hurt, because I'd trusted Tanya. She hadn't been mean to me in the past – apart from a few sisterly scraps – but at Cherry Road she became more distant, going off with her own friends and taking the mickey out of me. She didn't seem to care about anything any more – including me.

I also found it difficult sharing a room with her. Tanya was incredibly messy and would throw her clothes, and everything else, on the floor, while I liked to tidy up and have things neat. We often bickered over it.

At other times, we still felt very close, and in the early days we would sometimes cry in one another's arms, over how much we wanted to go home. We stuck up for one another too. One day, when one of the other girls punched Tanya over some argument, I stormed in, shouting at the girl to go away or I'd hit her.

Jamie seemed to settle in all right too. He didn't mind his new school and made friends with a couple of the other boys. We got on OK, though sometimes he still blamed me and Tanya for landing us all in care by telling about Terry. 'Why couldn't you just have shut up?' he'd say, before turning his back on us and walking off.

Cherry Road was situated on a really nice estate, much

smarter than anything I had seen before. The houses looked prosperous and well tended – they reminded me of Amber Smith's house back home. Some of them even had long drives, with smart cars parked on them. There was no litter anywhere. It was clean and peaceful and so very different from what I was used to.

I liked it, but I didn't feel very comfortable. I didn't feel I fitted into this posh area, or the clean, nicely kept children's home. I wasn't good enough. I felt like a visitor from another planet – the dirty, rough planet on the other side of the universe. And I didn't know how to change or adapt.

For most of my first year there, I gave the staff a really hard time. I broke the rules, answered back, threw things and had tantrums. I was fine as long as one of the staff was giving me their full attention – in fact, I lapped it up. If Craig or Melanie played a game with me, or took me for a walk and talked to me, I loved it. But the minute they stopped, I began behaving badly. I didn't care about the punishments – what was a bit of extra washing-up after the beatings I'd had in the past? I thought their punishments were daft.

Tanya was the same. She found it hard to fit in and made life difficult for the staff. But she had the ability to make friends, and once she got settled at the local high school, she had her own crowd of friends, both inside and outside the home, and spent her time with them.

Mum wasn't allowed to visit us for a few weeks, to give us

time to settle in. When she did come again her visits had to be supervised, as they had been at the beginning at Cranley. The staff at Cherry Road wanted to do their own assessment.

All three of us were thrilled to see her, and once again she was sweetness itself, telling us how much she'd missed us and that she was fighting to get us home. She said she knew she hadn't taken care of us properly, but that she had changed and when we came back everything would be different. She stayed for an hour, and came back again two weeks later. After a few weeks, she was allowed unsupervised visits, and these were to be twice a week – Wednesdays after school and Saturdays.

We were really happy about it at first. But we were often disappointed. Mum was now a fifty-minute drive away, and she told us it was too difficult to come by bus, so she could only come when John was free to drive her. She often missed the Wednesday visit and sometimes Saturday too. It wasn't unusual for her to stay away for three weeks before coming again.

Gradually, Tanya began to lose interest in Mum's visits. She was absorbed with her friends, and perhaps she'd had enough of being let down by Mum. It was no fun waiting to see if she'd turn up or not, and so Tanya didn't. She went out, and if Mum came, it was just me and Jamie waiting for her. I don't know whether this hurt Mum; she never said much about it.

If John drove her, he and his kids would stay out in the car park while Mum came in to see us. At the end of the visit, she'd say, 'Come out and say hello.' We did, reluctantly, knowing that we'd have to watch them all drive away together. I hated that more than anything – seeing them together, like a family, and feeling that I wasn't part of it any more. Afterwards, Jamie would be angry and I would be unsettled and distressed, and a staff member always spent the rest of the evening with me, trying to cheer me up.

Mum was incredibly insensitive about parading her new family before us. But despite this, she still seemed to be trying to win us back. She would tell us that she was going to all sorts of meetings and doing her best, but they still wouldn't let us come home. The trouble was she made us feel that it wasn't her fault – so it must be ours. We must be doing something bad to stop them from letting us go home.

Although she was trying, Mum made some silly mistakes. The first was when she bought me a video player and some videos for my first Christmas at Cherry Road. Penny and Melanie were horrified when they saw them – they were all 15- and 18-rated films. They took them away and I never got them back again, so that was my present from Mum gone. I did get little presents from the staff – and we all got some extra pocket money too. But I missed having a present from Mum.

Soon after this, Mum did something really strange. She'd been to visit, and was about to leave. She gave me a hug – and then suddenly turned her face and bit me on the cheek. It really hurt, and I began crying. Mum said she'd only been playing and hadn't meant to do it, but when I looked in the mirror there were teeth marks in my cheek. The staff were shocked when they saw them – and Mum's visits were stopped for several weeks. We were allowed to phone her during that time, but she never had much to say. She didn't ask about us, and if she talked about anything it was her and John and the kids and how well they were all getting on. I would end the phone calls feeling unwanted and shut out of her life. Why would she want me when she had Shaun and Kelly living with her?

At Cherry Road the staff persevered with me. Melanie was my favourite. She often spent time with me, reading to me, making up poems and playing board games. She had grey hair, even though she wasn't really very old, and she would tell me about her two children. Sometimes she gave me a pound to clean her car out on a Saturday, and then she'd walk to the park or the shops with me.

Ted was fun too. For some strange reason he was scared of monkeys – or at least he said he was. We kids used to love playing tricks on him – planting toy monkeys on his desk or in the loo. He would always yell at the top of his voice when he saw them, and we'd fall about laughing.

At weekends, the staff would organise things for us to do. We went swimming, roller-skating, to theme parks and on nature trails. We played games, went on outings and learned about the world outside, and I loved it. I had never done things like that before; my world had always been so confined and narrow. Now I was being offered the chance to explore and learn, and I soaked it up. Ted would shout, 'Right, swimming, get your things,' and I'd race round collecting my stuff and be first into the mini-bus we all went round in.

I was given £1.40 a week pocket money, and Melanie or Craig would walk me to the shops so that I could spend it. We also got a monthly clothing allowance of £17, which could be saved up for a big spending spree. I got some pretty clothes that were actually appropriate for a ten-year-old – another first.

I was still wearing make-up, including eye-liner, mascara and lurid-coloured eye-shadows. But when my eyes became infected and I got a couple of styes, Melanie came and talked to me and told me I needed to stop wearing make-up, especially on my eyes. I was still reluctant, because the older girls did, so she compromised, saying that I could put on a bit of blusher and lip gloss at the weekends, but strictly no eye make-up.

Gradually, I was learning how to be a child of ten, rather than an over-precocious doll. But I didn't see it that way for a long time. I thought make-up and short skirts and cigarettes would make me feel grown-up, and I resented having them all taken away.

Anna still came to see the three of us every week. But I stayed angry with her for a long time, and refused to talk. As far as I was concerned, she had put me here, instead of sending me home, and I wasn't going to forgive her. She tried hard and was always patient, but I wouldn't give in. I told her I hated being in a home and wanted to be fostered. She came back and said she was trying to find me a foster family, but the authorities wanted us to stay together, and it was hard to find a family to take the three of us. She didn't give up, but she never did find a family. If she had, I'm not sure whether I would really have been pleased or not. I told myself I hated Cherry Road, but though I refused to admit it for most of the first year, I actually liked it there. I felt safe and cared for. The rules made sense, and I knew where I was with them, and what would happen if I broke them. And we had a lot of fun. The meals were amazing. I couldn't get over all the new dishes whose weird and wonderful names I had never heard before – beef stroganoff and kedgeree were regularly served up, and I loved them. And the staff sat down to eat with us and seemed to genuinely like us and enjoy our company. Even though there were so many of us, it felt like being part of a family.

Unlike Cranley, Cherry Road had no lock on the kitchen door, or on the cupboards and fridge. If we needed a drink or a snack, we could go and get one, though we were supposed to ask permission. The only problem with this was that I had no self-control and I couldn't stop snacking. They say that over-eating can be brought on by a craving for love, and in my case I think it was true. I was always sneaking things from the fridge and stuffing my face, enjoying the comfort of it – until I felt sick. Of course I began to pile on weight. I had always been a little bit plump, but now I began to be quite tubby. The other kids in the home laughed and called me fat, and so did some of the kids at school. I hated that, but I couldn't stop eating.

Every night one of the staff would write a short report on the day's happenings, and then we would be asked if we agreed with it or wanted to write something ourselves. I liked this, as it gave us an opportunity to say things on paper that we normally wouldn't have had the courage to say out loud. Most of the time I would just read what they had written and write nothing, but I gradually got braver about adding my own notes. When they had written that I had been naughty, I would often say I didn't agree with them, even though I knew they were right. I liked being able to give my opinion, and disagree, without getting into trouble. I had never been able to do that before.

If the only influence on me had been the staff, I might have settled far more quickly and given up misbehaving, arguing and acting up. But, like many kids, I was very influenced by the other kids around me. And because they were all older, I wanted to be older too.

The girl I admired most was called Sandy, and she was fourteen. All the boys seemed to like her and she had lots of friends. She looked so grown-up, with her hair all done up nicely in a bun and a lot of carefully applied make-up. I wanted to look like her and be like her.

I did my best to get her attention, showing off and trying to copy her. And when she dared me to bunk off school and go and steal stuff from the local supermarket, I did – several times. For some reason, I stole loads of mouth-fresheners. Perhaps that's why, when I gave her most of the stuff I took, it still didn't impress her.

Frustrated, I tried harder, being more and more annoying, hoping to get her and the other older kids to notice me. But it didn't work. They carried on ignoring me, and in the end I gave up.

Chapter Ten

A few months after we arrived at Cherry Road, I turned eleven, and the following September I moved up to the local high school. Instead of coming into a school halfway through a term – as I had at the last two – I started with all the other kids, and I hoped that would help me make friends. But it didn't. I endured constant taunts and jibes, first about my weight and then about living in a care home. School is one of the hardest places in the world to be when you are different.

I made friends with a girl called Lucy, who lived near to Cherry Road. We got on well in school, and I really wanted to play with her outside school too. I used to go over to her house and ring the bell and ask her mum or dad if she could come out to play. But they always said no. Lucy wasn't the sort of girl to play out. She was protected and cherished, while I was the wild kid from up the road. I didn't give up for ages, I kept on calling, but in the end I realised she was never coming out.

The teachers at this school tried hard to encourage me. They would tell me I was a bright girl who could achieve things if I wanted to. The staff at the home said the same things. They'd tell me I was bright and pretty. I would retort hotly that I wasn't, but secretly it gave me a little warm buzz, like an inner smile, to hear them say those things. No-one had ever said anything nice about me before. But I was so unused to hearing anything good about myself that it was hard to believe them – I thought they were just trying to be nice.

I was now at school with Tanya and Jamie again, and they were regularly bunking off, so I began going with them. I was desperate to get away from the taunts of the other kids, and I was always easily persuaded – anything Tanya wanted to do, I wanted to do too, because I thought it was grown-up. Tanya and I would go to the bus station and hang about until nine thirty, then use our dinner money to buy a day-rider ticket, which meant we could ride the buses all over Manchester all day. We'd sit on the top of a bus, seeing the sights, and then make sure we got back in time for the end of school. We were only eleven and fourteen, yet no-one ever stopped us or said a word, as we got on and off buses all day.

We had real adventures; every day we saw something new. Then, one day, when Jamie had bunked off with a mate, Tanya said to me, 'Why don't we get the bus over to see Mum?' We did, and I couldn't believe how easy it was. Until then I'd thought of Mum as being miles and miles away, but in fact she was only a couple of bus rides distance from me. We worked out what buses to take and just turned up.

The first time we went home I was so happy. I hadn't been

to our house for almost two years, so it felt very strange, walking up the road and seeing it there. Nothing had changed on the outside, except that it was scruffier than ever.

Mum came to the door and looked amazed to see us. When she heard we'd bunked off, she chuckled; she was always pleased by anything that got one over on the authorities. She made us a cup of tea and asked us how we were. But after that she seemed to lose interest, and she went back to watching the telly.

Though outwardly little had changed, the house didn't feel the same any more. John's kids were sleeping in our old bedrooms and I felt very weird and unsettled, knowing that there wasn't a place for me there.

Despite this, we bunked off and went home several more times. No-one ever found out, and we would just sit in the house all day with Mum or play out on the street with the other kids who hadn't bothered going to school that day. Mum would always stress that we mustn't say a word to the authorities or it would ruin our chances of being able to go back to live with her, and we made sure we got the bus back to Cherry Road in time for tea.

Although I still acted up and wouldn't admit I liked Cherry Road, I was becoming more settled. So when a couple of the older kids said they were going to run away I didn't really want to leave. But Tanya said she was going, so, desperate to be part of the gang, I said I would go too.

The escape was planned for a couple of nights later. I packed a few clothes in a carrier bag and waited for the midnight signal – a tap on our door. It wasn't hard to get out – a downstairs door had to be left with only an inside bolt on it, to comply with fire regulations. All we had to do was slip back the bolt and creep out. We walked and walked until eventually, at about three in the morning, we got to a garage about eight miles from Cherry Road. We went in, hoping to get a lift from someone who was stopping for petrol. There was a taxi driver there, and we told him we'd been to a party and needed to get back home. We gave him Mum's address, thinking we could all go there. He said he'd take us, and asked us to wait while he went to the loo.

A few minutes later a police car turned up and we realised the taxi driver had shopped us. Cold, cross and tired, we were driven back, to be greeted by a very angry Penny, who doled out punishments all round.

I ran away several more times, mostly with Tanya. I usually decided to go after I'd got into trouble and been stopped from watching TV. I hated having to go to bed before all the others and was always begging to stay up for an extra half hour. When the staff refused, I'd throw a strop and then think, 'Right, I'm off.' I'd ask Tanya to come with me and we'd wait until the middle of the night and take off again. The trouble was, after a couple of hours we'd be cold, tired and bored. A couple of times we walked all the way back and got back into bed and no-one ever realised we'd gone.

On one occasion I ran away alone, after Tanya dared me to and said that I was a wimp and too scared to do it. I felt I had to prove her wrong. So that night, off I went. I was always scared of the dark, and out in the middle of the night on my own, I was terrified. It was cold and very dark and there was no-one about. After a couple of hours, I couldn't stand it any more. I was bored and cold and tired, so I went back. The trouble was, it was still only eleven at night, the staff were still up, and Craig happened to be looking out of the window as I let myself back in, so I got caught. I was punished with extra chores for two weeks, but I didn't really mind; I quite liked all the attention and fuss. Melanie came to talk to me several times, asking me why I wanted to run away. I just said, 'Dunno' and in many ways that was the truth. I really didn't know, because life at Cherry Road was good.

Then another blow fell. Penny took me and Tanya into the office and explained that Jamie was to be allowed home again, but we were not. I felt betrayed. Why was Jamie going home and not us? Had Mum said she just wanted him? He had always been her favourite. Now he was going home, and would be part of Mum's new family, while we were left in care.

Penny explained that they didn't feel certain that Tanya and I would be safe, so we had to wait a bit longer. But I didn't understand that at all. I ran to my room and lay on the bed, crying my eyes out.

Jamie couldn't hide how pleased he was to be going home. He did try to be nice and tell us we'd be there soon ourselves. But neither of us really believed it. A couple of days later, Mum arrived to collect him. She came in and gave him a big hug and Tanya and I just stood and watched, feeling unwanted.

It took me a few weeks to settle down again after that. I couldn't stop thinking of Mum with John's kids and now Jamie, all settled in at home, while we were left to rot. Though in truth, we weren't rotting, we were actually quite happy and settled in Cherry Road. But I couldn't get past the feeling of being abandoned.

By the time I was almost twelve and Tanya was nearly fifteen, I had decided that we should both have boyfriends. I longed to be wanted and liked, and I became convinced a boyfriend was the answer. I knew boyfriends were supposed to be nice to you and pay you lots of attention. I began chasing the boys at Cherry Road around, asking them to find us boyfriends, although Tanya was more than capable of finding her own and had already had several. This got me into trouble with the staff, who said it was unacceptable behaviour for a girl of my age. They threatened to cancel Mum's visits if I didn't stop.

Mum was still coming – when she managed to get lifts – and she seemed to take pleasure in telling us about all the presents she was buying Jamie and all the fun they were having now that he was home. She'd already bought him a Sega Mega Drive and a music centre and all sorts of other things we would have loved. It only added to our belief that he was Mum's favourite.

A few weeks later, we were told that Mum would be allowed to take us out for a few hours at a time. At first it was only an hour, and we'd walk around the shops and go for a cup of tea. When all went well, she was allowed to take us for several hours, and eventually for a whole day. We were supposed to go shopping, or to the cinema, but as soon as she had us for the day, Mum just took us straight home. This was strictly forbidden, but the staff never found out.

Of course we'd already been home, when we bunked off school, so we were used to going there anyway. And, to be honest, although we'd wanted to go back so much, it was no fun at all. The moment we arrived, Mum seemed to revert to her old self and lose interest in us. She settled in front of the telly with a cup of tea and ignored us until it was time to drive back to the home. It was as if once she was back on home territory, she forgot about loving us and being kind and went back to being just the same as she'd been before. She was all smiles and cuddles at the home, but as soon as she was out of sight of the staff she'd be cold and distant again. She had kept saying she wanted us back, but when we were actually at home it didn't feel as though she wanted us at all.

She seemed irritated by our presence, and told us to go out and play. We were only allowed in to do jobs for her, or rub her feet or back.

After a few of these trips home, I began to be quite glad when Mum didn't turn up to take us out. It was boring hanging around our house, with nothing to do and no-one to talk to. John would be at the printers where he worked, his kids would be out playing, and Tanya and I just mooned around, feeling lost.

Jamie didn't seem happy to see us either. He hated having these new kids in the house and he blamed me and Tanya for it. He said that if we hadn't been taken away, after blabbing about Terry, then the other kids wouldn't have moved in. He'd only been back for a short while, but already he was in all kinds of trouble again, stealing and breaking into houses. Mum didn't mind, as long as he gave her plenty of the stuff he stole. He'd come home with armloads of sweets, cakes and cigarettes, and even things like tellys and videos. He'd sell those, and Mum would pocket at least half of the cash.

We all hated Shaun and Kelly being in our house, but I soon realised that they hated it too. And most of all they hated Mum. They thought she was a witch, because she was so horrible to them. She beat them, made them miss meals, and if they forgot to clean their teeth she made them brush their teeth with salt. They hid a knife in her pillow, hoping it would stab her when she got into bed. She found it when she fluffed the pillow up, and she was livid. It never occurred to her to wonder why they wanted to kill her.

John was a loving dad, and all this was putting his relationship with Mum under a lot of strain. And that made her even more irritable and tense. I used to go out onto the street and hang about, thinking that the kids at Cherry Road were probably off swimming or enjoying a fun outing and wishing I was there.

By this time I'd been at Cherry Road for over a year and a half and I was a much happier, calmer and less angry child than I had been when I arrived. The staff's kindness and concern had broken through the shell of my resistance and hurt, and I genuinely loved all of them. They would spoil me, giving me little treats or letting me do jobs to earn extra pocket money. I had stopped smoking and was gradually relaxing into being the child I really was, rather than the imitation adult I had been forced to be.

When all the bedrooms were redecorated, they even allowed me to choose my own wallpaper. The one I fell in love with was called 'woof'; it had little dogs all over a blue background. I was still sharing with Tanya, but luckily she approved my choice.

I had stopped stealing and running away and was far less disruptive. I had learned to keep to the rules and it was rare for me to be punished or get into trouble.

I had also made a friend, at last. A boy called Lee had arrived a few months after me. He was a skinny little kid in glasses, a little younger than I was. He had learned karate and we would play-fight, though he'd win every time. He was a joker and he made me laugh. We began hanging around together in our free time and it was nice to have a friend. Lee was there for about nine months, then one day he told me he was leaving to go home. I missed him a lot.

Even school was better. I was catching up and sometimes getting very good marks and I'd begun to make some friends. I was far more talkative and confident than I had once been. I no longer hung around the edges of the playground, and I joined in with the other kids' games.

Anna was still coming to see me and Tanya, though by this time it was only every couple of weeks. She monitored our progress closely and she told me how happy she was that I was doing well. I had long since forgiven her for sending us to Cherry Road – I understood by then that it wouldn't have been her decision alone anyway.

Mum was still visiting us, though she often missed one or two visits, and one day she told us that she had broken up with John. 'Couldn't stand his bloody kids,' she sniffed. 'The little buggers put ground-up tablets in my tea. Tried to kill me. Anyway, they're gone now and I'm glad. Best off without them.'

I pretended to be sorry that Mum and John had split up,

but I was actually delighted. I had always hated the idea of those other kids living in our house. I didn't blame them for hating Mum; I'd seen how horrible she was to them. But that didn't mean I liked them or wanted them around.

Then Mum dropped a bombshell. 'Been in touch with George,' she said. 'He's out of prison, living in a flat across town. We're thinking of getting back together.'

I was stunned. I had thought that George was gone forever. Now it seemed he was not only out of jail, but planning to move back into our house.

'Trouble is,' Mum went on. 'The social services busybodies are kicking up about it. They don't want me to take him back. He won't do anything wrong, I know he won't. But they won't give him another chance. They want me to give him up or they won't let me have you back.'

I could just imagine Anna's face when Mum announced she was thinking of getting back together with George. And I knew they wouldn't let us go home if he was there. I didn't want to – I was sure he would do terrible things to me for putting him in jail.

After that visit, I began to think that we might never go home. I felt very down; it really hurt to think that Mum would put George before me and Tanya.

So I was startled when Anna arrived one Friday afternoon, sat me and Tanya down, and asked us if we'd like to go home.

'Yes, of course,' we both said. 'But can we go?'

'Yes,' Anna smiled. 'We think it's time for you to go back. I'm going to take you tomorrow.'

This was very sudden, and I felt shocked. 'What about George?' I asked.

'Your Mum has finished with George and agreed to break off all contact with him. She's on her own with Jamie now,' Anna said. 'She really wants you to come home, and we feel sure that you're both going to be safe and well cared for.'

When Anna had gone, Tanya and I hugged each other. We were going home, at last!

That evening I told Melanie. 'Yes, I'd heard,' she grinned, giving me a hug. 'I'm so glad for you. We'll miss you.'

'I won't miss you!' I laughed. But that night, lying in bed, I realised that actually I would miss all of them at Cherry Road – a lot. And I wasn't even going to have a chance to say goodbye to everyone at school. The more I thought about it, the more uncertain I felt about going home. Of course I wanted to be with Mum and Jamie. But I couldn't stop the nagging doubts. Would it really be OK, like Anna said? Would Mum still love me, like she seemed to when she came to visit? She had never been like that at home, not even on our sneaked visits.

Of course, Anna and the staff at Cherry Road didn't know about our visits home. As far as they were concerned, we hadn't been back there for over two years. And we couldn't tell them without getting Mum and ourselves into trouble. So we kept quiet, and I squashed down my doubts and fears and looked forward to going home. Things would be different this time, I told myself, of course they would. Mum had fought all this time to get us back and that meant she loved us and would be nice to us.

The next morning, I was excited as I packed all my stuff up and sat on the end of my bed waiting for Anna. When she arrived, she came into my room to get me. Tanya was with her. 'We just need to have a final chat before we set off, Louise. Is that OK, love?' Anna said. I grabbed my bag and followed them to the small office where the staff usually went for their meetings.

Anna told us it was normal that we should be a little bit scared about going back home and not to worry too much if we felt nervous. She asked how we were feeling and we both said we were excited. 'That's good,' she smiled. 'Before you realise it you'll have forgotten all about us here. Now, let's go and say goodbye to everyone.'

We went through to the kitchen, where all the staff and kids were gathered, waiting for us. When I saw them, my eyes filled with tears. Had they really all come to say goodbye? I had thought we would be whisked out without a word from anyone, the way we had when we left Cranley. I looked around. Even the staff that weren't on duty that day were there.

Suddenly I realised how much they liked us and cared about us.

I turned to Tanya, who had tears running down her cheeks. That was it – I started sobbing.

Penny stepped forward and put her arms around us. 'Come on, you two, stop crying. It's meant to be a happy time for you both, not a sad one. Come on and show me your best smile,' she said. But there were tears in her eyes too. I held on tightly to her as some of the other kids came and hugged me.

Those kids had been our family for the last two years and despite all our differences and squabbles, we cared for each other. As they stepped forward, one by one, to hug me, I realised that they really did like me – for myself – and it felt special. This was what families should be like.

Last to come and hug me was Melanie – my favourite member of staff. 'You take care and have a great life,' she whispered.

'Thanks for everything,' I sobbed, as Anna took my arm and led me out to the car.

They all came to the door and we sat in the back, waving, as Anna drove down the street. My last glimpse of Cherry Road, as we turned the corner, was of a dozen waving hands and smiling faces.

The journey home seemed to take forever, and as we wound through the city streets, my stomach started to churn and I began to feel giddy and sick. It was real, we were going home, and though I had longed for this day, I was scared.

Beside me, Tanya was silent, and Anna was unusually quiet too, so we made the rest of the journey in silence.

As we pulled into our street, I saw Mum at the window, watching out for us, with Jamie beside her. Suddenly I couldn't wait to hug her, and to go into the house, knowing it wasn't just for a sneaked couple of hours, but to stay. I was home. The only funny thing was the car parked outside our house. It looked just like the one John, Mum's ex-boyfriend, drove.

When the car stopped, I jumped out. Mum opened the front door and I ran to hug her, with Tanya behind me. She put her arms round us, kissing our heads and telling us how happy she was to see us.

Anna came up the path, carrying our bags, which she'd pulled out of the boot. Mum let go of us and took a step towards her.

'That's as far as you go,' she hissed, snatching the bags from her. Then she pushed us through the door, followed us in and turned and slammed it in Anna's face. I felt upset and embarrassed. Anna had been so kind. But I didn't want to risk Mum's mood turning, so I said nothing.

We went into the living room – and stopped. There, sitting in a chair in front of the telly, was John. And beside him were Shaun and Kelly.

'Hello, girls,' John said. 'Nice to see you.'

We looked at Mum, who mouthed, 'Forgot to tell you, we're back together,' before telling us to sit down while she made us all a cup of tea. Awkwardly, we went in and perched on the sofa next to John's children.

'Where are they going to sleep, Dad?' Kelly said.

'Don't worry, we'll sort things out, there's plenty of room for everyone,' John replied cheerfully.

I suddenly twigged. John and Mum were not only back together, but he and the kids were living with her. My heart sank. Where would we all sleep? There would be five kids in the house, but there were only four beds.

Mum soon let us know. 'You can share the bottom bunk with Kelly,' she said to me. 'Tanya can have the top.'

I had no choice. But that night, squashed into the bottom bunk with Kelly, I lay staring into the darkness, thinking about Cherry Road. Anna had been wrong when she said I would soon forget them. I knew I never would. I wouldn't forget how welcoming they were, and how they kept on trying to get through to me, even when I rejected them. I wouldn't forget the trouble the staff took to play with me, talk to me, listen to me and show me I mattered.

I had changed at Cherry Road. I had been liked and wanted, and that had made me into a different person. I had found confidence and self-belief. I didn't want to go back to being scared all the time and crushed and hopeless.

I wanted coming home to be the best thing ever. But deep down I knew it wasn't. What I didn't know yet was just how big a mistake the authorities had made in sending me back there.

Chapter Eleven

At first Mum was really nice to us. She was calm and friendly, she didn't snap and she didn't make me do jobs for her. In fact, she couldn't do enough for us – she made meals, baked us cakes and even played games with us.

It lasted three days.

After that, she lost interest, and went back to watching TV and asking me to make her cups of tea and snacks. I didn't mind doing that. But I found it really hard with so many of us in the house. There wasn't even room for all of us to sit in front of the TV in the evening. I often ended up sitting on the floor.

It was obvious that Mum still didn't like John's kids. She put up with them because she wanted John around, but as soon as he was out of the house she snapped and swore and lashed out at them and they scuttled out of her way.

Tanya and I had to start school again and we were switched to the local comprehensive, Parkstone, which was up the road. This time there was no social services budget for our uniforms. I was supposed to wear black trousers or a skirt with a white shirt and a burgundy sweatshirt. I ended up wearing Jamie's old school sweatshirt with a pair of black track bottoms with holes in them and a t-shirt that had once been white but was now a dirty grey.

It was halfway through the summer term, so I had to join the year eight class, which had been together all year. I soon realised that most of my old classmates from the junior school were there. I had been away for three years, so it was strange seeing them all. But the worst part was that they knew I'd been taken away and put into care. From the day I got there I was taunted about that – and my weight. I was still plump, and the kids lost no time in calling me every fat name under the sun. The one that really stuck – and that hurt the most – was Fatty. Mum had always called me that, Tanya and Jamie picked it up and now everyone else did too.

Not surprisingly, I was miserable at school. It wasn't quite as bad for Tanya – she was slim and pretty, and she'd had friends in the past who were glad to see her again. So she seemed to fit back in, while I felt I was unwanted and out of place.

Jamie was fourteen, but he'd stopped going to school. In fact, it soon became clear that he was out of control. He was stealing stuff all over the place, breaking into shops and houses and taking whatever he could grab. Mum encouraged him to do it. She liked the stuff he brought, and threatened to shop him to the police if he didn't give her half.

His stealing was fine by her. But what she didn't like was that he was also violent and aggressive. He started sniffing butane gas, used for cigarette lighters, and he was high a lot of the time. It made him unpredictable and dangerous. He and his mates used to sit around the living room flicking dried peas at me with a catapult. They really stung when they hit me. Or he'd whip me with towels, shrieking with laughter when I ran away.

One day I went in to find him with a mate, throwing darts around. When Jamie spotted me he started throwing them at me. I tried to duck out of the way, begging him to stop, but he laughed and then lobbed a dart which went straight into my foot, where it stuck. I pulled it out, but I was in agony. I fled to my room, in tears, as Jamie howled with laughter.

He got violent with Mum too, and sometimes she'd lock him out of the house. But she'd always let him back in; he was still her favourite. Not like Paul, who was out of the young offenders' institution by this time. Mum told us cheerfully that he was living in a hostel across town. She didn't seem at all bothered and, far from being concerned or wanting to help him, she laughed about the idea of him stuck there on his own.

I felt sad and worried when I heard about it. I didn't want to be around Paul, but I didn't want him living like that. Surely someone could find him a proper place to live and help him get back on his feet? I ventured this to Mum, who exploded. 'What do I care, bloody waste of time he is,' she spat. After that I didn't mention Paul again.

Mum bought Jamie an old car, even though he was much too young to drive. It was parked outside the house, and he would spend hours sitting in it. It wasn't long before he taught himself to drive, and after that he'd roar around the estate, brakes screeching.

He'd already been in trouble with the police several times, for theft and breaking and entering. So far he'd got off with fines, and Mum had borrowed the money to pay them. The day came, though, when he got violent once too often and Mum decided she'd had enough. She told him he had to move into the garden shed, because she wasn't having him in the house any longer. He didn't mind – he thought it was a laugh. He put an old carpet and his bed in there, rigged up an electrical extension and set up a stolen TV and hi-fi, so that he had a pad to take his mates to.

He was well out of it, because in the house things were tense and difficult. Mum and John weren't getting on at all, because of the way she treated his kids. One of them was always in tears and I heard John and Mum arguing – his voice low, hers shouting that she'd had enough of his brats.

In the end, it was John who'd had enough. Six weeks after we got home, Mum hit Shaun across the head and sent him flying. It was the last straw. Calling Mum a 'cruel bitch', John and his kids moved out that day.

Before he went, he came to see me and Tanya in our room. He had always been nice to us, and I could see he was upset.

'I'm sorry, girls,' he said, with tears in his eyes. 'It's not work-ing out between your mum and my kids. We've got to go.'

He could have said that Mum was nasty to his kids all the time; he was being considerate because she was our mum. No doubt he realised that with his kids gone, we would get the brunt of her temper, and felt for us.

I was sad too, because I liked John. He was patient and wouldn't bite our heads off for no reason at all. He would listen if we wanted to speak to him and was always ready to give us time. Though we hadn't known each other well, I would miss him.

The split sent Mum into self-destruct mode. Over the next few weeks she began drinking more and more. She also began taking anti-depressants. When she'd been drinking she could go one of two ways – either she would be happy drunk and making all sorts of promises about what we were all going to do, or she would be violent and aggressive. We never knew which it would be, though the latter was more likely.

Mum took to spending most of each day in the local pub. When she did come home it was either with some man she was seeing – most didn't even last the week – or she'd bring back a crowd of drunken people who sat around our house drinking, smoking and eating.

They would drink extra-strong cider, known as Mad Dog. Mum used to put a hole in the lid of the can and drink it through the hole; she said, 'It gets ya pissed quicker.' They were all smoking cannabis too, and giving each other blow-backs – where you take in the smoke and then blow it into someone else's mouth – in front of me and Tanya.

It began to feel as if our home was no longer our home. Day after day, Mum sat around the living room with her 'mates', most of whom wouldn't have given her the time of day if she hadn't given them somewhere to hang about and drink. I'd come in from school to find fourteen or fifteen people sitting around in a cloud of smoke, all with cans in their hands and glazed expressions, the TV blaring in the middle of the room while they stared mindlessly at it, or laughed at nothing.

'There you are, Fatty,' Mum would slur. 'Get us something to eat, will ya?' I'd go to the shop for potatoes and bread and then head into the kitchen to make plates of chip butties for them all. I'd do my best to clear up, emptying ashtrays and collecting up the cans, while one or other of them would crack a joke about me and they'd all roar with laughter. Then Mum would try to embarrass me by talking loudly about sex, and telling them all I'd never had a boyfriend. I cringed, wishing she'd just leave me alone and let me be invisible, but she seemed to enjoy taunting and humiliating me.

Around this time, I had my first period. I told Mum that morning, and when I came in from school she announced it to all the people she'd brought home from the pub, while I raced up to my room, hot tears of humiliation running down my cheeks.

The following month I whispered to Mum that I needed sanitary towels. 'You'll have to use toilet paper,' she said. 'Or borrow something from the neighbours. I need my money for booze.'

I had no choice – I went over to a neighbour who had a daughter a bit older than me, and asked to borrow a few towels. I was so embarrassed I could only look at the floor.

Most of the people who Mum brought back were men, and a lot of them were younger than her. But I don't think she cared who they were, she just wanted company, and anyone would do.

One of them was a hugely fat man who lived up the road. He stank of body odour and was covered in scabs. I could hardly stand the sight of him, but he and Mum would sit swigging from cans and laughing at me. He would be really horrible to me, joking about how ugly I was. I hated him.

Mostly, I stayed away from him and all the rest of them, staying in the kitchen and only going through to the living room when Mum called for me to make more food or get some cans from the fridge. Sometimes I ended up cooking tea for ten people.

I had stopped smoking at Cherry Road. With caring adults around, I hadn't felt the need to try to impress by smoking. But now that I was home, everyone around me was doing it. One day Mum, drunk as usual, taunted me: 'Come on, Fatty, if you think you're so clever, let me see you smoke a cigarette

– properly. You've got to smoke the whole thing and take it all down.' She cackled with laughter and so did the assorted layabouts slumped around the room. Red-faced and desperate to fit in, I did. I felt horribly sick as I inhaled drag after drag, but I finished it.

Then I passed out.

Mum left me lying on the floor and ignored me. I came to a minute or two later, sick and dizzy, and crawled upstairs to bed, shrieks of laughter ringing in my ears.

I didn't give up. I tried again – on my own – and within a couple of weeks I'd become a smoker. I hoped it would help me fit in, but it didn't really.

In this climate, with my self-esteem on the floor, no friends and an endless supply of chips, my weight ballooned. By the time I had turned thirteen, a few months after I came home, I was a size sixteen. This only made me feel more different than ever. Everywhere I went I felt inadequate and inferior to others, singled out and awkward. I was becoming more and more miserable, and ate to try to feel better. But the more I ate, the more different I felt – and the more I got picked on.

I began to feel paranoid. I was sure people would look at me and know what had happened to me – that I'd been abused and been in care. I had no-one to talk to – after one or two visits to make sure we had settled in, Anna had stopped coming and I felt more alone than ever before.

The truth was that, even to people who didn't know about

the past, I did look different. Not only did I have no school uniform apart from baggy track bottoms and a grubby t-shirt, but while the other kids wore trendy trainers or nice shoes, my ancient trainers had holes in the soles and the toes. And my school bag was a battered carrier bag, into which I had to cram my books and whatever I had to take to school that day. Even the nice kids would giggle as I walked past them.

Then one day I made a friend. She was called Susie, and she was a year younger than me. I knew who she was because her brother was in my class. We got talking one day on the way home, and struck a deal. I had to go home for lunch each day, while she got dinner money. So we agreed that she'd spend her money on ten cigarettes, which we would share, and I would make us both a sandwich at home. Every lunchtime we'd walk back to my house, where we'd eat and smoke in the kitchen until it was time to go back to school.

I really liked Susie – we got on well – but her parents didn't like me. They lived in a much smarter house than ours, away from our estate, and both of them worked. Susie wore a smart school uniform, and they didn't want her mixing with a plump, scruffy kid like me. So we kept our friendship secret. But even though it was restricted to lunchtimes and the odd evening when Susie could slip away, the friendship meant a lot to me. It was about the only good thing I had.

It was after Mum found a new boyfriend that I found out Anna hadn't stopped coming after all. It turned out that she was still seeing Mum once a fortnight, but Mum always engineered it so that Anna came when we weren't around, or she would walk to the social services offices in town for the meeting, just to make sure Anna didn't see us. It was malicious; she hated the fact that we liked Anna and she still resented Anna for taking us away. She often said to us, 'You're all little bastards. It's social services fault, they've ruined you.'

Mum's new boyfriend, Reg, was pale-faced and skinny, with lank, mousy hair. He smoked a lot and his teeth were brown and rotten. He claimed benefits and worked cash-in-hand, selling hot dogs and burgers outside city-centre pubs. He and Mum seemed to get on well – at any rate, they had a lot of sex and were always nipping upstairs – and he'd hand his takings over to her when he came in, so she liked the extra money.

He started hitting me almost as soon as he arrived. He was always doing it, sometimes even throwing me to the floor. He didn't need a reason; anything I did would be excuse enough.

It came to light when the school nurse gave me a routine examination and saw there were numerous bruises all over my body and on my face too. She must have called social services, because Anna came round a day or two later and took me out for tea.

I was really glad to see her. And when she asked me about the bruises I told her that it was Reg. Anna looked worried, and later she spoke to Mum about it. Mum said she knew about it and that he only hit me when I 'deserved it'.

Perhaps I might have been taken back into care at that point, except that Reg walked out on Mum a week or two later, so the problem was solved.

Now that Jamie was in the shed and John's kids had gone, we had a spare room. So Mum invited Auntie Coleen's eldest son, Andrew, to move in. He was about nineteen and he paid rent and helped with jobs about the house and garden. He was friendly enough. But after a couple of weeks he began going out with Jane, a young single mum who lived across the road. Jane was twenty-three and she had a two-year-old son, Kevin.

It was Mum's idea to get me to babysit Kevin – unpaid – so that Jane could come over to our house and be with Andrew. Of course, he could have gone to her place, but Mum wanted them both to join in her endless parties. So I was dispatched to mind the toddler.

I didn't mind – it got me out of the house, and Kevin was quite sweet. But they began leaving me there for longer and longer. Jane had made up a bed so that I could stay over, and I would often wake to find that she hadn't come back yet, and I had to give Kevin breakfast. One day I woke to a loud bang. Kevin had got up and stuck his fingers into a socket, and fused the whole downstairs. At twelve, I was too young to know how to look after a small boy. But no-one seemed to care. At one point I was left looking after him for two weeks, while Jane and Andrew lived it up at our house. The only time I was allowed home was to collect more clothes.

By the time I had been home for six months, I felt life couldn't get much worse. I was fat and wore rags. I was the butt of everyone's jokes. I dreaded school so much that I hardly ever went. And the only value I had to anyone was as a babysitter or to make butties and cups of tea. They all thought I was a waste of space, and that's how I felt about myself. I wished every day that I'd never come home from Cherry Road. I missed everyone there so much. I would lie on my bed thinking of them, wondering what they were doing and imagining what I would be doing if I was still there.

I hated everything about living back at home. Mum had conned everyone. She didn't love us at all.

Then one afternoon Mum called Jamie, Tanya and me into the living room and made an announcement that left us staring at her with our mouths hanging open, not sure we had heard right.

'I think it's time you all saw your father,' she said. 'I've been in touch with him, and he's coming over – tomorrow.'

Chapter Twelve

I had often thought about my real dad, and wondered what he was like. Mum had painted a horrible picture of him over the years, telling us he was a monster with three staring eyes, who scared anyone who saw him, a vicious, drunken man with a terrible temper, who would lash out for no reason, and who hit her and us kids. We were all better off without him, she told us, and we believed her.

But sometimes I couldn't help wondering where he was and what he was doing, and if he really was that bad. I dreamed about a dad who would love me and be glad I was his and come and get me, and in recent years I'd had this dream almost every day. I wished that I could see for myself what my dad was like, but I never really expected to – and certainly not through Mum. So when she announced that she'd been in contact with him, the questions came thick and fast from the three of us.

We wondered why Mum had contacted him, after so many years. 'Just thought it was time,' was all she'd say. But the truth was that without a man by her side to ease the burden, Mum was finding the responsibility of us children a bit too much. She'd left us to George, and then Terry. With no-one else around, she wanted our dad to step in and help. And of course she was short of money and hoping for a handout.

It turned out that our dad was living less than three miles away. I was pleased that we'd be meeting him at last. But I couldn't help feeling worried. 'You said he was horrible and wicked,' I said to Mum, nervously.

'He's not that bad,' she said, gulping down her coffee.

I had believed her so completely that it took me a while to digest the new information – perhaps our dad was not a monster after all. I wondered about the three eyes, but decided not to push Mum by asking too many questions.

She had arranged for him to come to the house the next day, a Sunday, which didn't give us long to get used to the idea. As the rest of the day passed, I began to feel excited. I was finally going to see my father. I'd be able to fill in some of the blanks in my life, and that felt good. All the other kids I knew who didn't live with their dads at least saw them – in most cases every week. We were the only ones I knew of who had no dad in the picture at all.

I wondered why Dad had agreed to come. After all, he'd left and not bothered to contact us for all these years. If he'd cared about us, surely he would have been in touch? What had Mum said to persuade him to come over?

I thought of all the times when having a dad around would have helped. He could have rescued me and Tanya, instead of letting us go into care. He could have had us over to his house, instead of leaving us with Terry and George. Where was he when all those awful things were happening? I had so many questions running through my head, but I knew I probably wouldn't have the nerve to ask him a single one of them. I wanted everything to be nice when he came, I didn't want to risk pushing him away. But deep down I was angry with him, upset that he had left me and not bothered to come back.

I spent most of the next morning sitting in my room, waiting and wondering. The tension in the house was so high that we were all restless. Jamie and Tanya were both pacing around and Mum was drinking cups of tea non-stop.

As the clock ticked, my stomach was full of butterflies. What would this mystery dad be like? Jamie had been three and Tanya four when Dad left, so they could remember him a little better. Jamie was especially eager to see him again and watched out of the window.

He was due at eleven and, bang on time, the doorbell went.

'He's here,' I heard Jamie shout.

I got off my bed and walked to the top of the stairs, staring down at the front door as a shadow appeared on the other side. It looked big and I swallowed. I still expected to see three eyes when he walked in. But when Jamie opened the door, I was shocked. The man standing there looked clean, smart, rather scared – and very ordinary.

I stared at him, thinking, 'Where's his third eye?' But there was no sign of it. He just had the regular two eyes everyone had. He was tall, with fair hair and brown eyes. He wore smart trousers and a short-sleeved shirt and I thought he looked quite friendly.

He stepped inside and forced a smile. Behind him was a lady with blonde shoulder-length hair. Was she his wife, I wondered. If so, she looked rather old.

'Hello,' he said, looking at the three of us, who stood lined up in the hallway. 'This is your Nan, Maureen.' I realised that Dad had brought his mother. I could see how nervous he was – he probably needed a bit of support.

'Hello,' smiled Nan. She looked kind, and I did my best to smile back, but I felt it came out looking all wrong.

'Right,' Mum said, grabbing the kettle. 'I'll make some tea – you all go and sit down.' I looked at her in surprise. She never made us tea.

We all trooped into the lounge and sat around the drop-leaf table. Jamie, Tanya and I sat in silence, as Dad and his mum tried to make polite conversation, asking us about school. Mum brought us all tea, and we sipped it nervously.

After a few minutes, I decided to speak. There was something on my mind.

'What do we call you?' I said to him, blushing.

'Call me whatever you want,' Dad replied, smiling at me. The trouble was I wasn't sure what I wanted to call him. 'Dad' seemed odd, because I didn't even know him. But what else was there?

Mum kept busy, offering biscuits and topping up drinks, as we all looked at one another.

Gradually, we began to thaw out, but it was hard going. Tanya, Jamie and I all found excuses to leave the table and go upstairs or out to the kitchen for a few minutes at a time, just to escape the tension.

After an hour, Dad and Nan got up to leave. He delved into his pocket and pulled out an envelope, which he laid on the table.

'There's fifteen pounds in there for each of you,' he smiled. 'Get yourselves something nice with it.'

My eyes lit up thinking about what I could spend my money on. New clothes, some make-up, jewellery, sweets; I could probably get all of them with that much.

'Thanks,' I said, smiling at Dad. Jamie and Tanya thanked him too.

'I'll be back again next week, if that's OK with all of you,' he said.

'Yes, great,' Mum said. We all nodded.

Mum shut the door behind him and turned to us.

'If you think you're getting this money, you got another think coming,' she said, grabbing the envelope from the table. 'This'll do me for bringing you lot up, without a single penny from him.' And she ripped open the envelope and stuffed the money into her pocket.

We stared at her. How could she be so unfair? Our dad had given us that money. I wanted to run after him and tell him that Mum had taken it. But I knew she'd make me suffer if I did. So I stomped upstairs, feeling gutted and knowing she would spend it on more supplies of Mad Dog cider and cannabis.

Later that day, I said to Mum, 'You told us he had three eyes. But he didn't.'

She roared with laughter. 'You didn't believe that, did you?' she said. 'I was only joking.'

I thought about Dad a lot in the week that followed. The meeting had been awkward and tense, but he'd tried hard. I decided we should give him a chance.

The following weekend, he came over again. This time he came alone, and he brought sweets for us. I was glad – Mum wasn't likely to take them away. None of us mentioned that she'd taken the money when Dad teased us about how we'd probably spent it all on sweets and chocolate.

Mum left us in the kitchen with him, so we were all a bit more at ease. Dad told us about his partner, Sandra, and said he would like us to meet her once he'd got to know us a bit better. He explained that he had to come over to our house, as he didn't have a car and the bus we would have to take to get to his place went on a long roundabout route and took forever. But he said that he'd decided it was time he learned to drive, and he'd already started lessons.

He was nice, and I thought he must like us if he was bothering to learn to drive so that he could take us to his house. I couldn't see why Mum had hated him so much. I wondered whether he had really done all the bad things she accused him of. But whatever he had or hadn't done, I was just happy to have a dad and to feel that, at last, I was like other kids. I decided that I would call him 'Dad'. It had begun to feel right.

For the next few weeks, Dad came over to see us every Sunday. Mum would behave nicely in front of him, making the tea and then leaving us to chat to him, and as we got to know each other, we all became more relaxed.

About six weeks after Dad started coming over, Tanya turned sixteen. She wanted a party, and Mum agreed. Tanya wanted Dad to come, and to our surprise Mum said yes.

On the day, we all dressed up and Tanya's friends came over, along with our aunties and a few of Mum's gang. Dad turned up with Nan and his sister, Auntie Allie, with loads of presents for Tanya.

Dad seemed to get on well with everyone, and I felt proud. I kept thinking, 'I've got a dad, and he's nice.' It felt so special.

Dad passed his driving test soon afterwards and bought a car. The next weekend he came to collect us and take us out for a drive. Jamie was off with a friend, so Dad took me and Tanya. And, to my surprise, he headed for the area where Cherry Road was.

'Why are you bringing us here?' I asked.

'I love this area,' he said cheerfully. 'I often come here. It's so pretty, and there's a lovely market in the village. Do you know it?'

We told him that it was where we had been in a children's home, and he looked sad. 'I'm sorry, girls, I knew you'd been in care, because social services told me, but I didn't know it was here. Do you want to go home?'

'No,' we told him. 'It's fine.' And it was. I liked seeing the area again and so did Tanya. I couldn't help wondering if Dad had been there when we were at Cherry Road. Perhaps we'd even passed him in the street.

After that, Dad came every weekend to take us out, and we drove all over the place, exploring different areas. Then came the day when he said, 'Would you like to come to my house?'

'Yes please,' we squealed. I couldn't wait to see where he lived. His house was a three-bedroom semi, like ours, but his was in a nicer area and it looked smarter. Standing in the doorway, smiling, was a very plump woman with a warm face and a big smile.

'Well, it's good to meet you,' she said, giving all of us a hug. 'I'm Sandra. I can't tell you what it means to your dad to be seeing you again.'

I was puzzled. What did she mean? If it was so important to him, then why had he stopped seeing us? I wanted to ask, but still felt too unsure of myself – and him – to risk it.

We had a lovely time that day. Sandra was kind and

motherly and made us a big meal. She had three grown-up children of her own. She and Dad had met soon after he split from Mum, so they'd been together for over twelve years. Dad worked in a bakery and Sandra worked in a café, cooking and waiting at tables. They seemed to be really fond of one another and happy together.

After that, Dad took us over to his house every weekend and I loved it. Jamie and Tanya didn't always come. They would be off with their friends, and Tanya had a boyfriend called Kevin and spent all her time with him. So it was often just me. I was so starved of affection that I lapped up the cuddles and hugs Sandra gave me, and when Dad asked me if I'd like to stay the night one weekend, I happily agreed.

I slept in a large spare bedroom which was light and spacious. It was never normally used, so it only had a bed in it, but I liked it because it was so clean and all mine.

At bedtime I gave Dad a kiss and cuddle and then Sandra took me up to bed. She tucked me in, stroked my hair and kissed me goodnight. She made me feel I was special to her and after she'd gone I lay in the dark, remembering her touch on my hair and thinking that no-one had ever touched me like that before.

The next morning they offered me a choice of cereal, toast or a cooked breakfast. I asked for a bacon sandwich. I loved them and never had one at Mum's as bacon was expensive and if we ever had any it was only for Mum.

I loved my stay, and asked to come again. Before long I was staying over every weekend. The arrangement suited everyone: Mum was glad to have me out of the way and Dad and Sandra seemed to like me being around. As for me, I felt at last I had found people I could trust, and I wanted to be with them. Dad wasn't much richer than Mum, but he gave me time and attention, we did things together and he didn't shout at me or get angry, and that meant the world to me.

I couldn't get over how different things were at Dad's. I had the run of the house and was free to help myself to food in the kitchen. I would make myself toast and jam and coffee and sit on the sofa with them, in my pyjamas and dressing gown, grinning like a Cheshire cat. Dad and Sandra must have thought I was easily pleased, but to me toast and jam and coffee was luxury. Mum would never allow me things like coffee; she always said it was too expensive and only she and the guests could have it. I wasn't allowed jam either. I had to make do with real basics unless Mum was feeling in a particularly good mood, or the shoplifters had been round selling stolen goods and she had got some bargains.

Mum always seemed to be agitated by my very existence, but at Dad's it was so different. He and Sandra seemed happy for me to be there. They gave me a say in what we watched on TV and asked me what I'd like to eat and where I'd like to go. I felt wanted in a way I never had before. Sandra had her part-time job in a café near their house and Dad would take me in there to wait for her to finish.

I loved watching Sandra working behind the counter, making sandwiches and burgers and pouring cups of tea and coffee. She must have seen how transfixed I was by it all, because one day she yelled over to me, 'Don't just stand there, young lady, get this apron on and give me a hand.'

I didn't need to be asked twice. I grabbed an apron and went behind the counter and Sandra told me to butter a pile of bread.

I loved my stint in the café, so after that day she would take me to work with her most Saturdays and let me help her serve the chip butties and burgers. She'd give me two pounds for helping, and then on the way home we'd go to the shops for chocolate cake and sweets. Back at home, we'd sit on their shocking-purple sofa and cuddle in front of the TV.

When Sandra wasn't at work, she and Dad would often take me shopping in town. We'd wander round the shops, just looking, or buy things they needed for the house.

I never asked for anything; I already felt I had so much from them. So when Sandra steered me into a shoe shop one day I looked at her, puzzled.

'Come on,' she grinned. 'I've seen you staring at those trainers over there. Let's see if they've got them in your size.'

I felt so excited I was almost giddy. I had longed for a pair of pretty new trainers, but never thought I could have them.

I'd had to make do with ugly old second-hand ones ever since I could remember. I'd had new shoes at Cherry Road – but never trainers.

I sat staring down at them as I tried them on, not wanting to take my eyes off them for a second.

'Well, do they fit?' Sandra asked.

'Yes,' I beamed, looking up at her. 'They're great.'

'Better wear them right now then,' Sandra smiled, heading over to the till to pay.

My tatty old shoes were thrown into a bin outside the shop as we left. I couldn't stop looking down at my feet – I was afraid that if I did the trainers might disappear. For the next few days I bumped into everything in my path – people, bollards, dogs and post-boxes.

Being with Dad and Sandra was like having a taste of a different life and I wished it could last. I always felt upset when I had to go back home again, but I didn't dare suggest I went to live with them – I didn't know if Mum would agree, or if they would want me around all the time.

Dad's mother, Nan, often came over to their house to see me. It was she who told me how hard they had all tried to see us in the past.

'We never gave up,' she said. 'Your dad longed to see you, and so did I. We tried all the time. We sent birthday and Christmas cards, and took presents round. Your mum wouldn't give any of them to you.

'Your mum and dad had fallen out, but that was no reason to bar us from seeing you. We wanted to, so much. Your dad tried again when you went into care. But your mum always told social services that he was violent and asked them not to let him have any contact.

'We couldn't believe it when she got in touch to say she wanted him to come over and see you. It was like all our Christmases had come at once.'

I felt shocked and amazed to hear that Dad had wanted to see us all along.

Later I plucked up the courage to ask Dad if he really had been violent. He looked very serious and paused, trying to find the right words. 'I didn't behave well,' he said at last. 'Your mum and I were fighting all the time and I lost it a few times. I'm not proud of that. But I loved you kids; I want you to know that. Your mum and I were better off apart, but I was absolutely gutted when she said I couldn't see you.'

Hearing this turned my world upside down. I sat alone in my room thinking about it for hours. Our lives might have been so different. George and Terry might never have been able to hurt us the way they did. We might never have been in care, if only our dad had been in our lives.

If only Mum had let him see us.

Chapter Thirteen

Jamie was still getting into all kinds of trouble, and inevitably it came to a head. He'd got away with fines and warnings so far, but when he was caught stealing yet again, he was told that this time he would probably get a custodial sentence.

In the hope that it might make a difference, Mum asked Dad to let Jamie come and live with him and Sandra, and Dad agreed. Jamie was delighted, and moved straight away. I couldn't help feeling a bit jealous – I'd have liked to go and live with them, but instead Jamie got to go because he'd been thieving and breaking the law.

Once Jamie was there, I saw less of them. Dad and Sandra had their hands full with him, and although I was still welcome, Dad wasn't able to come and get me as often, and the atmosphere there was more strained. My happy weekends helping Sandra in the café and cuddling on the sofa afterwards became more and more rare. I felt sad and hurt that, once again, Jamie seemed to be more important than me.

I was spending most of my time at home – where Mum was still partying every day with the people she met in the pub. She still seemed to be on a path to self-destruction, drinking heavily and wearing flimsy, revealing clothes. She was flirting with lads half her age, wearing baby-doll nighties with her dressing gown hanging open. She would parade around the room, cackling with laughter, a fag hanging out of her mouth, telling filthy jokes and dropping innuendos and of course the lads she invited over would be winking at each other with big grins on their faces.

I was so embarrassed that I was quite happy to go and make drinks for all of them, or act as gopher for her, just to avoid having to watch.

Mum was also taking more drugs. She was still smoking dope, and now she had started using hallucinogenic 'magic' mushrooms. Jamie had brought some home, and Mum thought they were great. After he left to go to Dad's, she got someone else to bring her some. She'd eat them and then start laughing her head off in a really scary way. She tried to get me to take some too, but I was too scared. In the end I nibbled one, just to make her happy, but it didn't do anything to me at all – to my relief.

Tanya had dumped her boyfriend, Kevin, and seemed to have a new one every week. Mostly they were older lads, in their early twenties, and even though Tanya was still just sixteen, Mum let her sleep with them at home. We were in separate rooms by that time, because Jamie had gone, and Tanya had a double bed in our old room. She'd disappear upstairs with boys quite openly, and come back down an hour or two later, grinning.

I didn't want to be sleeping with boys the way Tanya did, but I was jealous of how popular she was. All the boys flocked around her and didn't even seem to notice me. I was still very podgy and shy, while Tanya was gorgeous and confident.

Then one day she disappeared. She hadn't been going to school for a while, so she spent her days out and about with various friends. We never knew where she was, but she always came home. Until one day she didn't.

The next morning I told Mum that Tanya hadn't come in. Mum didn't seem worried. 'She probably stayed at a mate's,' she said, yawning. 'She'll be back later.' But Tanya wasn't back later, and she didn't appear the next day, or the next.

It was social services who alerted the police. Anna was away, so another social worker came to check on us because we weren't at school, and heard that Tanya hadn't been seen for a few days. By the time the police came round, Mum had cleaned the place up and was all motherly concern.

I was worried sick about Tanya, imagining she'd been kidnapped or murdered. Why else was there no word from her? If she was all right, surely she would let us know? But then, I thought, perhaps she wouldn't. Perhaps she would think that no-one would really care.

When the police and social services weren't around, Mum didn't seem worried at all. I wondered sometimes whether perhaps she knew where Tanya was, and just didn't want the authorities to find out.

It was twelve days before they found her, living with a twenty-five-year-old boyfriend, the boyfriend's mother and her girlfriend, in a high-rise block of flats. She didn't want to come home, and as she was sixteen they couldn't force her. Mum certainly wasn't bothered. But a couple of weeks later Tanya came back, her face bruised from where her boyfriend had hit her during a fight.

Once Tanya was back, things carried on just as before. Mum was drinking, smoking and carrying on with younger men. Tanya was out most of the time, or taking boys up to her room. As for me, I was miserable. I'd started to feel a bit better about myself when I was spending time with Dad and Sandra. But with Mum poking fun at me, calling me Fatty and treating me like a slave, my confidence plunged and I felt down in the dumps, lonely and in the way.

Like Tanya, I had stopped going to school. By the time I was thirteen, I had more or less left. I just couldn't face the taunts, the name-calling and seeing people laughing at me. I was overweight and wore hideous clothes and was a sitting target for every bully. The teachers didn't help me and, even though I wasn't stupid, I was behind because I'd missed so much schooling. It seemed easier to give up on it all. No-one checked up on me or tried to get me to go to school, so I just sat at home. Sometimes I sat with Mum and her friends, but most of the time I was upstairs in my room, feeling that no-one in the world wanted me.

When she wasn't partying at home, Mum was in the pub. Her favourite, the Angel Inn, was a few minutes from us, just off the estate. She would arrive there wearing stiletto heels and plastered with make-up and often spent most of the day there, drinking and joking around with the other regulars.

I didn't mind her being in the pub – at least the house wasn't full of people sitting around expecting me to make them tea. But it meant I was on my own even more, mooching around and wondering what to do with myself. Sometimes I went down to the pub with Mum and sat quietly in a corner with a packet of crisps, just so that I didn't have to be on my own.

Most of the people in the pub were really friendly and some of them would come and say hello to me. But I never found it easy to chat or join in; I would blush and look awkward, until they gave up.

The pub was run by a couple, Gavin and Sheila. They were really nice and would often bring their three-year-old daughter, Lauren, down from the flat upstairs, where they lived. I would sit and cuddle her and play with her, and Mum suggested they might want me to babysit when they were busy and both had to work behind the bar. They jumped at the offer, and after that I often spent evenings upstairs at the pub, especially at weekends, playing with Lauren and putting her to bed. They didn't pay me, but I didn't mind – I loved looking after her and wished that I could have a baby of my own to care for.

Sheila was nice to me, but it was Gavin who was really

friendly towards me. He would often pop up to see if I was OK, bringing me some crisps and lemonade from the bar. Sometimes he'd stay and chat and I loved the attention. I thought he was really good-looking and developed a bit of a crush on him, even though he was much older than I was. But I kept it to myself – he was married and, besides, I was sure he would only think it was a joke if he knew.

When Mum met yet another new man, Craig, I didn't think he'd be any different from the others who'd come and gone. But Mum swore he was special and within a few days he'd moved in with us. He seemed all right. He was pleasant to me and he and Mum were always draped over one another, but it all seemed a bit hasty. Then one day, a couple of weeks after they'd met, Mum asked me to babysit at the pub so that Gavin and Sheila could go out with her and Craig for a few hours. I didn't know where they were going, but it didn't really matter, I was happy to babysit anyway.

When they got back, Mum seemed really excited and Gavin began pouring drinks for all of them. 'Guess what?' Mum said, coming over to where I was standing holding Lauren. 'We've got married! We just came from the register office – Gavin and Sheila were our witnesses.'

I didn't know what to say. I wanted to be glad for her, but she'd known Craig for two weeks. And she hadn't bothered to tell me she was going to marry him – or to invite me. Or Tanya or Jamie, come to that.

'Great, Mum. Congratulations,' I managed, before turning to take Lauren back upstairs. If Mum noticed that I was upset, she didn't care. They partied into the night and then went home and slept well into the next day.

Two days after the wedding Craig said he was just popping to the shops for something. 'See you in a minute,' he called, as he went out of the door. He never came back.

Mum wasn't worried at first, but when she checked with the pub and he hadn't been there, it dawned on her that he'd done a flit. She heard a few weeks later that he'd turned up on the other side of town, but she never managed to find him again, so she wasn't able to get a divorce.

Everyone at the pub had a good laugh over it. Even Tanya and I teased Mum. It had been a pretty crazy thing to do. Mum seemed to see the funny side. But then, a few days later, I came back home after babysitting to find Mum sitting alone in the front room, in the dark.

'Are you OK?' I asked her. She pulled out a note and handed it to me. I looked at it – it said that she'd had enough of trying to cope with us kids and how horrible we were, that we made her ill and she wanted to get away from us forever.

I was devastated and burst into tears. It felt awful to think she wanted to leave me. I couldn't help feeling that it was my fault and that I must be really bad. Yet when I looked up at her, she was grinning.

I wondered if she really hated us or if she'd written such

a cruel note because she really was broken-hearted over Craig. But if she was, she made an amazingly rapid recovery in the next few days. She seemed to forget she had just gained and lost a husband, and she went back to partying and hanging out at the pub.

I carried on babysitting. It was nice to have something to do apart from sitting around watching people drink, and Gavin and Sheila were always nice to me. In fact, Gavin was becoming nicer and nicer. I always felt like the ugly one next to Tanya, so when he started telling me how lovely I was, I felt great. He was popping up to see me all the time, and he began sitting next to me and holding my hand at first and then cuddling me and stroking my arm.

I wasn't sure what to do. I liked him, and he was nice to me, when most people barely noticed me. But he was older and married, and I didn't want to do anything wrong. So I sat, blushing and saying very little, unsure whether to run or not, while he paid me compliments, told me how gorgeous I was and got more and more amorous.

The trouble was that I thought Gavin was wonderful and different from the men who had hurt me when I was little. I would have done anything for him. I didn't see that he was a grown man in his early thirties grooming a thirteen-year-old girl. I just thought he was lovely because he was nice to me and wanted to spend time with me. I was the perfect prey.

Then one day he told me that he and Sheila were going to look after a pub in Wales for the weekend, to give the owners a break. They wanted me to go along with them to babysit. Mum was going to look after their pub while they were away, so everything was taken care of. I thought it sounded like an adventure, so I said yes.

In the car on the way up I sat in the back, next to Lauren, who was strapped into her seat. Sheila was in the passenger seat and as the hours passed both she and the toddler fell asleep. I became aware that Gavin was looking at me in his rear-view mirror. Time and time again I saw his eyes were fixed on me, and I became more and more uncomfortable. Why was he doing that? I just wanted him to stop.

When we finally arrived it was late. I helped Sheila put Lauren to bed, and then went to bed myself. I was sharing a room with Lauren, so that I'd be there if she woke.

I'd almost fallen asleep when Gavin appeared in the room. He told me how beautiful I was and that he had feelings for me. Then he sat on my bed and kissed me. I was so shocked I didn't know what to do. His daughter was asleep next to us, his wife was downstairs in the pub, and if I screamed or made a fuss she would hear. So I did what I had always done – I tried to pretend it wasn't happening.

After a few minutes, Gavin heard a noise and said, 'I'd better go, but remember, it's you I want,' and slipped out. I lay awake for the next few hours in turmoil. I wanted a boyfriend, like

Tanya, I wanted to be loved and I liked Gavin so much. But this was all wrong – Gavin was married, and too old. I didn't know what to do.

The next day Gavin kept winking at me, and when he passed me he would touch my bottom, or brush against me. When we went home, a couple of days later, I was relieved. But after a few days Sheila asked me to babysit. 'We're going to be really busy,' she said. 'Can you stay over? Then we needn't worry about keeping you up late.'

I agreed, and she showed me the spare room, where she'd made up the bed. I didn't mind staying – it was a cold night and I didn't want to have to walk home if Mum was staying on late. But in the back of my mind there was a nagging worry about Gavin. Surely he wouldn't try anything – would he?

The evening passed quietly. I put Lauren to bed, watched some TV and went to bed myself. Sheila had brought me up a drink and some crisps and there had been no sign of Gavin.

The next morning I woke in the early hours, around dawn. Suddenly the door to my room opened and I saw a shadow in the light from the hall. It was Gavin, wearing only his shorts and t-shirt, holding a finger to his lips to indicate that I should keep quiet. He walked over and sat on the edge of my bed, stroking my hair away from my face, and then leaned over and kissed me. Within minutes he had climbed in next to me and was rolling on top of me. Frozen with panic, I didn't dare say a word as he forced himself inside me.

Then the door banged open and the light was switched on. Sheila stood there, her face a mixture of anger and surprise. Gavin leaped from the bed and I lay rigid, my heart pounding so hard I thought it would explode.

'What are you doing?' she said, looking from Gavin to me.

'Shit,' Gavin whispered under his breath. 'Louise had stomach ache and I was just seeing if she was OK,' he said lamely.

The next moment, Sheila launched herself at him, hitting him, screaming and crying.

'What? On top of her in bed,' she yelled. 'You dirty bastard, she's a child.'

I hoped she would know I hadn't encouraged him, but I was soon proved wrong.

'Get out of that fucking bed now,' she yelled at me, dragging the covers off and then lunging at me with her fists. 'You dirty little slut, get the fuck out of my house.'

She turned to Gavin. 'And as for you, I'm calling the police straight away,' she shouted. She went towards the phone, but Gavin grabbed it, begging her to calm down and talk it over.

I stood with my back against the wall, still in my pyjamas, rooted to the spot. All I wanted to do was get out of the house and back home with Mum where I would be safe.

Sheila finally got hold of the phone and called Mum.

'You'd better get round here now and get your slag of a daughter out of this place before I fucking kill her,' she yelled down the phone. 'I've just caught the slut in bed with Gavin,' and she slammed the phone down.

She and Gavin disappeared into another room, and I was left there on my own, wishing a hole would appear and swallow me up.

Ten minutes later Mum arrived. By that time Lauren had woken and was crying, and Sheila was screaming at Gavin.

'You stay away from my daughter,' she yelled. 'You're never going to see her again.'

Mum grabbed my arm and dragged me out. She had a taxi waiting outside and we both got in. We went home in total silence. Mum didn't even look at me, and I didn't dare speak, or try to explain. I felt so confused. I hadn't done anything at all. Gavin had come into my room and got into bed with me, yet I was being blamed.

Back home, Mum marched me through the front door and up the stairs and then shoved me angrily into my bedroom.

'You're a disgrace and disgusting. Stay in your room all day and I'll deal with you tomorrow,' she shouted, slamming the door behind her.

I crawled into bed and lay crying for a long time. I wished I could turn back the clock and do something differently, but I wasn't even sure what. I curled up and held my knees tightly against my chest, gasping and crying as quietly as I could.

I was still crying by the time night arrived. I cried myself to sleep.

Chapter Fourteen

The next morning Mum ignored me, walking away when I went into the kitchen and slamming the door behind her. A few minutes later she came back in and told me I was grounded for the next two weeks. I never went anywhere anyhow so the grounding was pointless and didn't worry me. What did hurt was the look on Mum's face as she told me I had brought shame on the family and was a slut and a slag. I sat silently as she shouted at me. I wanted to curl into a small ball. I needed her to hold me and tell me it wasn't my fault and that everything would be all right. I wanted her to say that Gavin had taken advantage of me and was wrong. When she didn't, I began to doubt myself. Perhaps it was me, after all. I was the bad one, I thought. By the time she had finished laying into me I felt I would be better off dead.

I stayed at home for the next two weeks, mostly in my room, venturing out only to eat and use the bathroom. I felt dirty and shamed and lost. I had liked Gavin and the attention he gave me – so did that make me guilty? Why did my own mum always blame me, even when other people hurt me? I didn't want to see anyone or go anywhere. Just curl up in my bed and cry.

Jamie's court case was due, and Mum wanted to go. He was pleading guilty, so she didn't have to testify. She missed Jamie and hoped he would get off with another fine and come back to live with us.

Neither Tanya nor I went to court with her. She didn't ask us to go, and we thought she'd arrive back with Jamie that afternoon. But when she came home, she was alone, and her face was like stone.

'Bastards,' she said. 'Those bastards have sent him to a detention centre. Six months, he got. All for nicking a few bits and pieces. He should have got a fine, or community service. Those pigs had it in for him. I'm going to the pub,' and she stomped out again.

Mum had told me she could never go back to the Angel Inn after I had shamed her. But within days of the incident, Gavin and Sheila had split up and left the pub and new landlords had taken over. She made sure I knew that it was all my fault, that I had broken them up. But at the same time I could see she was pleased, because she could go back there again.

That's where she headed after Jamie was sent down. After she'd gone, Tanya and I looked at one another. We both knew Jamie had had it coming – he'd been thieving for years, and fines had never stopped him. But we were sorry too. We loved Jamie, and now he was gone, just like Paul.

A few weeks later Mum met a new man in the pub. Alan lived right next door to it – perfect for Mum. She fell for him in a big way and they started seeing one another every day. He was a bit older than Mum, reasonable-looking and friendly; he was very popular at the pub. He had a job and drove a nice car. So it was hard to work out what he saw in Mum. Perhaps it was just that she was lively and loved a party. Whatever it was, they quickly became an item, and from then on Mum was glued to his side.

I liked Alan, and the relationship actually seemed to calm Mum down a bit. She'd been moving from one man to another for months, so I was glad she seemed keen and hoped she'd stick with him. He was nice to me, and life was a bit easier with him around.

I couldn't help wishing that I had a boyfriend of my own. Mum, despite her size and the scars, had no trouble attracting men, and Tanya seemed to have five at once. All I wanted was one, but no-one had shown any interest in me at all, and I was beginning to think they never would when I met Daniel.

I don't know who brought him to our house. He'd never been before, but he appeared at one of Mum's parties one night and sat quietly on the sofa, holding a can of beer. I thought he looked really nice – he was over six foot, with a nice smile, dimples and dark brown hair and eyes. He looked fit and muscular and had big hands – I wondered what his job was.

It didn't even cross my mind that he might be interested in me. I ended up sitting next to him on the sofa because that was the only space in the room. So when – without saying a word to me – he took my hand, I was thrilled and shocked. I sat, my hand in his, neither of us looking at the other, wondering if he'd meant to hold my hand or had done it without even noticing.

We didn't say more than a few words to one another, and I realised he was as shy as I was. Sneaking little glances at him, I decided he was lovely. I couldn't believe he would really be interested in me. But he was – he stayed right to the end of the party and then, when I walked out into the hallway with him to say goodnight, he kissed me. It was my first proper kiss, and I felt so grown-up. Then he said, 'I'll come and see you again tomorrow, if that's OK?' I nodded; it was more than OK.

When he'd gone I wanted to dance around the room. Someone liked me! Someone wanted to see me tomorrow! And not just any old someone – a really nice-looking bloke. I couldn't imagine why he wanted to see me, but he did, and I felt so happy.

The next evening he arrived at six, after he'd finished work. He stayed all evening, the two of us sitting on the sofa, holding hands and watching TV. I was still only fourteen and was so nervous that I sat bolt upright, stiff as a board, for most of the evening. But Daniel didn't seem worried. At ten or eleven he kissed me goodbye, said he'd come the next day, and walked back to the house he shared with his parents, a few streets away.

That was how it went from then on. Daniel, who was eighteen, worked for a furniture removal firm, lugging crates, beds and chairs in and out of vans. After work every day he came over to see me and we spent the evening together. We never went out, we just sat together – him with a beer, me with a cup of tea – watching TV or chatting. If Mum was having a party we joined in, and if Alan was there, seeing Mum, the four of us would sit together.

Within a couple of weeks everyone accepted that Daniel and I were an item. I felt so happy that someone liked me. And I liked him – he was quiet, like me, and didn't ask anything of me. I knew he would come round every evening and being able to count on that gave me confidence.

Things seemed to have settled down. Tanya was seeing a boy named Danny and was usually out with him, Mum was happy with Alan and was doing a lot less drugs and being less crazy, and I had Daniel. I still saw Dad and Sandra some weekends, but now that Daniel was around, I didn't stay the night with them.

Then one day there was a knock at the door. It was a debt collector, threatening to take our furniture if Mum didn't pay the money she owed. Mum shoved him out and slammed the door.

'It's that bloody money I had to borrow to pay Jamie's fines,' she said. 'I haven't got it.'

By that evening she had come up with a plan. We would

do a flit and move in with Alan. Amazingly, given that they had only known each other for a few weeks, Alan seemed quite happy about it. So Mum, Tanya and I packed all our stuff into cardboard boxes, shoved them into the back of Alan's car once it was dark, and left the house we'd lived in for most of my life.

I wasn't really sorry to go, even though it was so sudden. So many bad things had happened there. As I looked back at it one last time, before we drove away, I half hoped that all the unhappy memories would stay with the house.

Alan lived in a maisonette. It was newer and smarter than our house. I got my own room, overlooking the Angel Inn, and Tanya had the room next door. It took us a few days to get used to the place, but I began to think we might be OK there. It was closer to where Daniel lived, so he carried on coming over every evening, just as he had at home. Alan liked him, and was happy for him to come – they would share a beer together and watch football on TV.

I settled in, but Tanya didn't like being at Alan's and wasn't getting on with Mum. She was rowing with her all the time, blaming her for us being taken into care. One evening Mum dragged Tanya off the sofa by her hair, screaming at her that she had no right to judge. Within two weeks of us moving in, they'd had an even bigger row and Mum kicked Tanya out. 'Don't think you'll be coming back,' she spat, throwing a bag of Tanya's things out of the door after her, 'because you won't.'

Tanya, who was now just seventeen, had dumped Danny and was seeing a boy called Pete, a friend of Daniel's. Pete had been in the navy but had been discharged after his leg was injured. He had a flat of his own, so Tanya went to live with him. Tanya and Mum refused to make up, but I used to go round and see Tanya. Mum didn't seem to mind that and I liked it round at Pete's place, because it got me away from Mum's constant demands and criticisms.

By the time I had been going out with Daniel for over a year, he still hadn't asked me to sleep with him. He always treated me with kindness and respect; it was as if he knew that he needed to be patient with me and wait for the right time. I hadn't told him about the things that had happened to me in the past; he had never pressed me on anything and I was grateful. He seemed happy to spend every evening with me, hold hands and kiss, and I was happy with that too. His gentle approach was like an antidote to the cruel, abusive treatment I'd suffered before and his loyalty and patience helped me to trust him, when I had never been able to trust any man before.

When he told me, one day that summer, that he was house-sitting while his parents and sisters were on holiday and wanted to throw a party, I was really pleased. I thought it would make a nice change from sitting in front of the TV. We asked Tanya and Pete and a few other friends over, got some beers in and sorted out some music.

As we were getting everything ready, Daniel put his arms round me and asked me to stay with him that night. I thought for a moment, and then said I would. I wasn't sure how I felt about having sex. After so many awful experiences, I couldn't really imagine it being anything other than an ordeal. But I knew Daniel would be kind and understanding, and I wanted to be with him.

I went back and asked Mum if I could stay the night at Tanya and Pete's place, so that I wouldn't disturb her and Alan when I came in, and she agreed. I didn't tell her the truth, because I knew she'd go mad and say no. For some reason – I never did work out why – she treated me and Tanya very differently in this respect. While she seemed happy for Tanya to be having sex with boyfriends from the age of fifteen and treated her like another adult, she didn't feel the same way about me. I was treated like a child, and she made it clear that I wasn't to sleep with boys. So far, I hadn't. Not because of Mum's rules, but because I hadn't wanted to.

But Daniel was different and I was determined to make my own mind up.

The party was fun, and it was very late before everyone left and Daniel and I went into his bedroom. I was nervous, and once I had got into the bed, I lay, stiff as a board. The hurt and abuse I had suffered in the past made me scared of sex and afraid to let him come close. In my mind, being loved wasn't a good thing; it led to pain and fear and suffering.

But when Daniel held me gently and told me he loved me, I knew he really meant it. He could feel my fear, and was patient and sweet. He tickled my back, kissed me, stroked me, and told me I didn't have to do anything I didn't like. When, eventually, we did make love, it was special, and I was so happy I had waited for someone who really cared about me.

The next morning we talked and laughed, ate breakfast and cleared up after the party. I stayed until lunchtime, then headed over to the pub, where I knew Mum would be, to get the keys to Alan's flat.

I was feeling happy as I walked into the pub. Daniel loved me, and that made me feel special. I knew I'd found a really good man.

Then I saw Mum's face.

She looked up at me as I walked over, and then stood up and said loudly, so that everyone around her could hear, 'Here she comes, the dirty little slag.' She threw the keys at me. 'I know what you've been doing, you little tart. You're disgusting.'

Mortified, my face burning with embarrassment and shame, I grabbed the keys and fled from the pub. Back in the flat, I lay on my bed sobbing. How could Mum humiliate me like that? Somehow she knew I had stayed at Daniel's, but I didn't really understand how she could be so angry about it. I had been with him for a year, he was my steady boyfriend. And I was fifteen – older than Tanya had been when she started sleeping with boys.

A few minutes later Mum arrived home. Her face furious, eyes blazing, she appeared in the doorway of my room. 'You're just like your sister, you filthy little slut,' she hissed. 'I saw you at Daniel's, so don't pretend you weren't there. You're a disgrace. I don't want you living here any more, so pack your things and get out – right now.

I was horrified. I had no money and nowhere to go. What on earth was I going to do?

Shaky and tearful, I put my things into a couple of bags. Mum followed me to the front door. 'That's right, get lost,' she shouted. 'And don't come back.'

She slammed the door behind me and I walked slowly down the street, lugging my bags.

I had no idea where I was going, or how I would survive.

Chapter Fifteen

After wandering around for a couple of hours, I went to the only person I could think of – Tanya. She and Pete only had a one-bedroom flat, but they said I could stay for a few days.

I called Daniel to tell him what had happened, and he came over. He was shocked, and told me he loved me and would do his best to find us a place to live together – but it would take time, because he didn't have much money. I was so glad that he wanted us to be together – I wanted to be with him too. But in the meantime I still had nowhere to live and no money.

Not only was there not much room at Pete and Tanya's, but Pete was making a living dealing drugs, and I felt really uncomfortable being around it. The whole place stank of cannabis, which was smoked day and night by all the people who came round, and I hated it. I needed somewhere else to go, and Tanya thought of Sally and Rod, the couple who were now living in Terry's old house, across the road from where we used to live. Tanya knew them and she went to see them and suggested they might like to have me as a lodger, for a bit of extra cash.

They agreed that I could move into their spare room, so I went to see social services, to tell them what had happened and see if they could help with money. Anna had left her job, so wasn't around any longer. I was sorry, because I'd known her so long and she'd been kind to me. But the woman who interviewed me was sympathetic and said she'd help.

While I was still at Tanya and Pete's, sorting everything out, the two of them decided it would be funny to put a tab of acid – LSD – into my tea, without me knowing. They had a few people round that evening, and Pete asked everyone if they'd like a drink.

Halfway through drinking my tea, I noticed that Tanya and Pete were watching me and sniggering. I knew they had spiked other people's drinks in the past – they thought it was a hoot and often did it – so I realised straight away what they had done.

I went into the kitchen and sieved out the little tablet, and then drank the rest of the tea, thinking it was safe. I didn't know that a fair amount of the drug would already have dissolved. Luckily, it wasn't the whole lot, so I ended up feeling a bit queasy and seeing things jumping about the room a bit, but I didn't have the full trip they'd planned for me. I was relieved, and glad that I was moving out the next day.

I went round to Sally and Rod's house with my bags in

the morning. It felt very strange walking back into the house where Tanya and I had spent so much time with Terry – and suffered at his hands – six years earlier. If there had been any other option I would have taken it. But there wasn't; I had to do it.

Sally and Rod were allowed to claim child benefit for me, and social services paid them £10 on top of that, towards my room and board. Mum was claiming family credit for me, and social services suggested that she give it to me, so that I had something to live on, but she refused to hand it over. So I had a place to stay and my meals, but apart from that no money at all.

Staying with Sally and Rod was not much fun. Neither of them had a job, so they were around the house all day. But they did nothing in the house either, so it was an absolute pigsty. The two of them sat and watched TV all day and smoked non-stop – it was like a re-run of Mum and George. They had a little blond-haired son called Duncan and he was lovely. I often sat and played with him. He was terribly skinny, which made his head look huge. And although he was two, he was still in nappies, not yet walking and barely talking. I was certain that he was undernourished. I often used to cook for all of us, just to make sure he got some proper food.

Some days I felt really down. I hated the muck and filth all over the house, but there was no way I could clean it all and keep it nice. It was just too big a job, and as soon as I cleaned anything Sally and Rod would mess it up again. They were complete slobs. The only day they got out of bed before eleven was the one they got their benefit money at the post office. Rod would have his weekly shower and then all three of them would set off on the bus. Once they'd got the money, they'd go to the supermarket and do a big shop, buying all kinds of goodies. Any money they had over would be spent on beer, so by the evening there would be no money left at all. We'd eat really well for three days, but by then everything would have run out, and we had almost nothing for the rest of the week, till payday came around again.

The two of them weren't easy company – they didn't talk to me much, so I kept to my own room most of the time. I hated the way they treated Duncan – they thought it was funny to teach him to swear and stick two fingers in the air. I didn't like watching, but I had nowhere else to go, day or evening, except round to Tanya's for a visit. I felt I had been pushed from pillar to post all my life, and here was one more place where I was being dumped.

At that point I had no picture of my future. I was sure I would never have an interesting job, or live somewhere nice, or achieve anything. I was a waste of space – that's what I'd always been told, and that's how it felt.

Dad came to see me. He wanted to know where I was

living, and to make sure it was all right. I hoped he might offer to have me move in with him and Sandra, but he didn't and I couldn't help feeling disappointed.

It was Daniel who made my life bearable. He had taken on extra night shifts at the factory to earn the money for a home for us, so he couldn't come round in the evenings. But he'd come over to see me every weekend, bringing cigarettes and a fiver, so that I had a little cash. He was a lifeline, when it seemed as though I had no-one else. When he left, at the end of a weekend visit, he would cry, because he hated leaving me in such a disgusting house.

I had been at Sally and Rod's for three long, depressing months when Daniel arrived one Saturday with a big grin on his face. 'I've got us a house!' he said, hugging me. 'Come on, I'll show you.'

I was so excited. I grabbed my coat and followed him out of the door. We caught the bus to an area just outside the estate, where there were rows of small terraced houses. Daniel led me down one of the narrow streets and stopped outside a house with a red front door. 'This is it,' he beamed. 'We can rent it for £55 a week, starting next week.'

I peered through the window. The living room looked clean and there was a carpet – but nothing else. 'It's brilliant,' I said, 'but it's got no furniture.'

'We'll get some,' Daniel said. 'I've got a mattress, so we've something to sleep on.'

That was good enough for me.

Just before we moved in, Daniel took me to meet his parents. I knew his sister, Joanne, who was a year older than me, from school, but I had never met his mum and dad. I knew they'd been worried that I was so young, so I was nervous and hoped they would like me.

They lived not far from the house we were going to rent. We went over for tea, and I liked his mum, Rose, straight away. She was round and cuddly, with dark hair and a ready smile. She welcomed me, fussing over me and insisting I ate plenty. She was a few years older than my own mum, and I felt instantly at home with her. She clearly loved her family and would look after and protect them all, no matter what.

Daniel's dad, Doug, was large and bald, with a big nose. He smoked and ate a lot, sitting in his armchair, while Rose did all the running around. But I could see that they got on well together.

Daniel told me later that his parents had met when Doug was twenty and Rose was nineteen. He'd been a roofer then, but he had a serious accident when he fell off a roof and injured his back and had never worked since. Rose worked in a clothes shop and had supported the family for over twenty years.

Doug was nice, but extremely tight with money. If you used the phone, he made you put 20p in a plastic tub and he would never pay for a bus or taxi or anything else he considered a luxury. He didn't drive and hardly ever left the house. Rose was the sociable one, with lots of friends, though she never drank or smoked.

I liked Rose and Doug and soon got to know them well. They helped us move in and gave us lots of bits and pieces for the house. When we first arrived, all we had was a single mattress, a quilt and a record player. But we didn't care. It was our own home, we could be together and do what we wanted and that felt so good that furniture just didn't matter.

I didn't tell social services I was living with Daniel. I was still fifteen and they wouldn't have allowed it. I told them he was a friend of my sister's boyfriend and had offered to rent me a room and, to my surprise, they accepted that.

Over the next few weeks I set about collecting things for our house. People we knew gave us all kinds of bits and pieces – pots and pans, curtains, even a sofa. The only thing we bought new was a washing machine that we ordered from a catalogue.

I really loved making the house into a home. For the first time in my life I had somewhere of my own I could enjoy. I put pictures up, arranged the kitchen, and cleaned everything so that the whole house shone.

I didn't even think about getting a job – I hadn't made it through school, so I had no qualifications, and I was still too young for most employers. Daniel and I were both happy with the situation, but I did get lonely. He was still working nights, to make extra money, so he was asleep most of the day. That meant we didn't get a lot of time together, and I would wander about, trying to fill my day with cleaning the house and window-shopping.

Once a week Rose would come round to see us and stay for tea. She would always check whether we needed anything and made sure we were all right. And on Sundays we would go round to her house for lunch. I liked feeling that I was part of a real family and I became good friends with Joanne.

A few weeks after we moved in, I realised my period was late. It had happened before, so I wasn't too worried. I decided to go swimming, because that usually seemed to bring it on. But it didn't, so I went to the doctor, who did a pregnancy test. I didn't really think it would be positive – I was still expecting my period to start at any moment – but the doctor rang back to say, 'Congratulations, the test is positive.'

I was stunned. I would be a mum at sixteen. As the shock wore off, I began to feel really happy. At last I would have something – someone – who was really mine. Someone I could look after and protect, so that they never had to suffer as I did.

When Daniel came home, I told him the news. He looked shocked. 'I hadn't thought about us having kids yet,' he said. The trouble was neither of us had thought about it – or about contraception. It hadn't even occurred to us.

Daniel said he would go with whatever decision I made. I

told him I was having the baby – there was no way I'd consider getting rid of it. 'Fine,' he said. 'We'll go for it then.'

When we went round to his parents for lunch that Sunday, we told them they were going to be grandparents. They were kind to us, and said they were happy, but we could see they were worried and unsure. Not surprising, given that Daniel and I had only been living together for a few weeks and I was underage.

Mum hadn't been in contact with me since she threw me out. I knew she sometimes heard how I was doing through Tanya, but we hadn't spoken. That hurt – I had hoped she would come and see me, and when she didn't I realised she must be happy without me. But I wanted to tell her I was pregnant, so I plucked up the courage to ring.

'Mum, its Louise,' I said. 'I'm going to have a baby.'

'Right, OK,' she replied. She sounded uninterested.

'Are you pleased?' I asked her.

'I'm not bothered,' she said. That really hurt. I decided not to contact her again.

I went round to see Dad and Sandra to tell them. Dad looked worried. 'Are you sure you know what you're doing, love?' he said. 'You're so young.'

'It'll be fine, Dad,' I said. 'I want this baby.'

A scan, a few weeks later, told us it was a girl. We were so excited. Knowing the sex somehow made it real. Daniel grinned at me. 'What shall we call her?' We went through all the names we knew. In the end we settled on Emily. We both thought it sounded beautiful.

I sailed through the pregnancy, feeling fit and well and fascinated by my growing bump. When I was five months pregnant, I turned sixteen. We had no money, so Daniel just gave me a card. I didn't mind. We had never celebrated birthdays when I was younger, because no-one cared. Now at least I knew it was because we had no money.

By the time my due date arrived we had decorated our second bedroom and filled it with everything the baby would need. Our families and friends all gave us baby presents, so we had enough nappies and tiny outfits for the first year.

I waddled around for a week after the due date, before going to hospital for a check-up. 'You've gone long enough,' the doctor said. 'We'll induce the baby in two days' time.' It was 1995 and we were in the middle of a long, hot summer. I was tired of feeling over-heated and heavy, so I was relieved that a date had been set.

I went home again and Dad came to see me. He popped over about once a week. He usually stayed for a cup of tea, chatted for a bit and then left. But this time he said, 'Come on, let's go and see Sandra and Nan.' We drove over to his house, where Nan was visiting, and we all got very excited talking about the birth. Then suddenly I felt a sharp pain, followed a little while later by another. I ignored it – I'd had pains before and they hadn't meant anything. And these weren't bad ones. But they carried on, and by the time Dad had taken me home, I was pretty sure this was it.

It was the middle of the night when I nudged Daniel awake and said I thought I'd better go to hospital. The trouble was we had no phone. He got dressed and walked to the phone box up the road to call for a taxi, while I got ready.

When we arrived at the maternity unit, they checked me over and said I was nowhere near ready to give birth and could go home again. But I said no, I preferred to wait in the hospital, rather than get a taxi home and then another one back again.

So I waited – and Daniel waited with me. All through the next day. Dad and Sandra came to see me, and so did Rose. She said I looked like a little girl, sitting in my hospital bed, screwing up my face every time a pain came.

My own little girl finally made an appearance in the middle of the next night. At one in the morning, on the day they had planned to induce me, Emily arrived. Small, red-faced and perfect. Daniel and I were both crying as we took turns to cuddle her. He was so happy that he rang his parents and woke them up to say, 'We've had the baby and it's the best thing that's ever happened to me.'

Daniel went home, but, unable to sleep, he soon came back again. The next day Rose arrived, along with Daniel's grandma and Joanne. They all cooed and fussed over Emily, taking turns to hold her, and I felt so proud.

As for me, I loved her with all of my heart from the moment I saw her. Something deep inside me felt complete, and I was certain that I would never be alone again, with this little soul to look after.

Chapter Sixteen

My baby was eight weeks old before Mum came to see her. She turned up out of the blue, just as I was wheeling Emily out of the house in her pram. I had an appointment to view a council house we were hoping to move to. We were struggling to make ends meet in the privately rented house and the council rent would be lower, which would give us a bit more spare cash.

I was shocked to see Mum. My heart was pounding and I didn't know what to say. I was afraid she had come to have a go at me. In the end I stuttered that I had to go out. She wasn't happy and she flounced off in a huff. I was hurt and disappointed. I wanted to show Emily off to her, but Mum barely stopped to look at her and she certainly hadn't brought a present. I was so disappointed. She'd finally made it to see her granddaughter and she'd taken offence because I had to go out. That was Mum – she had to come first, or there was trouble.

The council house was awful. It was a maisonette on the worst estate in the area. Half the houses had their windows boarded up because they'd been smashed by the local gangs and the front door was up a flight of concrete steps, with no lift. I looked at the housing officer who'd come with me and burst into tears.

They offered us a two-bedroom terraced house next. It was much nicer, so we said yes. We moved in when Emily was three months old, and Daniel's mum did most of the decorating for us. We made it really pretty.

A couple of months later, Mum showed up again. This time she had brought what she called 'her' new car – it was Alan's new car, actually, a white Rover. I admired it and we had a cup of tea together. Mum held Emily, and by the time she left, we'd called a kind of truce. But I didn't plan to see much of her.

Daniel and I settled down to family life. He worked hard and we lived very simply, barely ever going out, just staying at home and looking after Emily, happy to have our home and to be together.

Daniel's sister, Joanne, often came to stay with us at weekends. She was quiet and hard-working – she'd stayed on at school and did three paper rounds. When she was with us she would take Emily out in her pram to the local park, so that I could get a few chores done. She often spent her hard-earned money on little presents and treats for Emily, and I grew very fond of her.

We'd often go shopping together, and Emily and I even went to Butlins for a few days with her and Rose. Daniel couldn't get off work and Doug didn't want to come, so we had a girls-only break and I really enjoyed it.

Tanya was still with Pete, and six months after Emily was born, they had a son, Callum. They moved into a council house two streets away from us, so we were able to see a lot of one another and look after the babies together. But while Daniel and I had a very peaceful relationship and never rowed, Tanya and Pete's was turbulent and violent. They fought a lot. After one huge row, Tanya had stabbed Pete in the arm. The police had been called and he'd been taken to hospital, where he'd needed an operation on the tendon. Tanya wasn't prosecuted and the rows went on. On many occasions Pete punched holes in doors and Tanya threw cups and plates around.

They both took drugs, which fuelled their violent tempers, and they carried on right through Tanya's pregnancy. Thankfully, Tanya's drug-taking didn't seem to have harmed the baby. But when Callum was only a few months old, Pete got caught burgling a house. He was sent to prison for two years, which left Tanya alone with the baby. Lonely and broke, she started hanging around with a girl called Cheryl, a prostitute who was hooked on cocaine. She had a little boy, and Tanya babysat him while Cheryl was working. Soon Tanya had dumped Pete and was going out with Cheryl's brother, Gary. He was twenty-three and good-looking, with his dark hair tied back in a ponytail. But he was unemployed and spent most of his time taking drugs.

I worried about Tanya hanging around with Cheryl and Gary, and tried to warn her that they were trouble, but she wouldn't listen to me. She was so impressed by the money Cheryl made and all the things she could afford – though most of her earnings went on drugs, as far as I could see. I hoped Tanya would break free of them, but she thought she'd found the perfect best friend and boyfriend, and nothing was going to change her mind. She knew I didn't really like them, and she began avoiding me. I felt really sad – Tanya and I had always been close, we had shared so much, and I really loved her.

A few months later a neighbour told me that Tanya had gone on the game. She'd decided she wanted the kind of money Cheryl was earning, so she'd started work in a massage parlour. I was horrified. Could Tanya really have done that?

I went round to see her and asked her myself. She admitted it was true. 'What's the problem?' she said. 'I'm fine – it's good money. Gary looks after all the kids now, while Cheryl and I work.' She smiled, but the smile didn't reach as far as her eyes. They looked sad and empty.

There wasn't much I could say. I was frightened for her. She was still only twenty and her life seemed to be on a downward spiral. But when I argued with her, she told me to get lost.

I walked home feeling sad, and very alone. Mum wasn't interested and now Tanya didn't want to know me. I decided to put all my efforts into my new family. I wanted to give Emily everything I didn't have, and bring her up to have a good life.

The only member of the family I still saw from time to time was Jamie. He had moved in with a girlfriend, Sarah, and they were getting on well. But Jamie had got into a fight outside a nightclub and had been beaten up so badly that he had to have three operations. It took him a long time to recover, and he wasn't able to go back to his job as a warehouseman. I felt really sorry for him, but I was glad he had Sarah; she stood by him and seemed to really love him.

I loved being a mum, and Emily was an easy baby. But, even so, I was shocked when I found out – just after her first birthday – that I was pregnant again. I'd been on the pill since the birth, but I'd forgotten to take it for a couple of days, and that's all it took.

I turned eighteen when I was seven months pregnant. It didn't mean a lot to me. I was legally an adult, but I'd felt grown-up for most of my life. Dad gave me a fiver, as he always did for birthdays, and I got a present from Rose and Doug, but Daniel and I had so little money that he couldn't buy me anything. He earned £180 a week and our rent was £55. The rest went on food, bills, baby things and to his dad for cut-price groceries and the washing machine he'd helped us buy. We couldn't even afford to smoke most of the time.

Sophie was born in the spring of 1997. My waters broke at

two in the morning and the contractions started almost immediately. Daniel called Rose and asked her to come and look after Emily and then called an ambulance. This time I had an epidural and labour was a lot quicker than the first time. But afterwards the placenta wouldn't come away, so I was given an injection to help it along. The doctors warned me that it would make me sick, and it did. I was so ill that I couldn't hold Sophie – Daniel held her and cried with happiness, as I threw up all over the place.

Sophie was a big baby – and gorgeous. We were so proud of her. When I brought her home, Rose came to stay for two weeks, knowing that it would be hard for me to manage a toddler and a baby. She did everything she could to help, taking Emily off so that I could look after Sophie. After the two weeks were up, I had to manage on my own – but Rose came once a week, as she always had, and stayed to put the girls to bed.

At eighteen I was mum to two girls, and when Daniel asked me to marry him, shyly producing a ring he had bought, I was thrilled and said yes straight away. I'd gone from having no future to having one that seemed to be all mapped out. Daniel was steady, dependable and hard-working, when so many of the men around where we lived were out of work, or dealing drugs, or walking out on their girlfriends and kids. I felt sure he would never do that to us.

Daniel worked long hours, while I was left at home looking after the girls and, perhaps inevitably, though I hardly dared to admit it to myself, there were times when I felt a bit bored and trapped. I was so grateful for my little family, but it did sometimes feel as though I'd gone from childhood straight to middle-age.

I didn't have many friends or much money, so there wasn't a lot to fill my days. So I was glad to have one good friend up the road. Jody was a couple of years older than me, and she'd had a son just before I had Sophie. We got on well and we spent a lot of time hanging out with our kids. She helped to fill the void left by Tanya.

Jody's boyfriend, Phil, was nice too. Unlike Daniel, he was often around, and one day he casually asked me if I'd like to try some amphetamines. I wasn't sure what to say – I'd had no idea he had drugs. I looked over at Jody. 'Go on,' she laughed. 'I take them sometimes – it gives you a buzz. Try it when the girls are in bed.'

It turned out that Phil was getting his drugs from Pete, Tanya's ex, who was out of prison and back dealing. I said I'd think about it. I was shocked – and a bit intrigued too. If Jody took them, perhaps there wasn't really any harm? And I wanted to know what the 'buzz' was like. Was I missing something great?

I didn't take the drugs then. But a few weeks later I decided to say yes. It was a stupid thing to do. But I was eighteen and not very wise. I didn't think about what it might lead to. I hadn't taken drugs since the day Tanya and Pete had spiked my tea. Now I convinced myself this was a bit of harmless fun. I swallowed a couple of pills and the effect was amazing. I felt warm and bouncy and chatty and really good about myself. I couldn't believe it.

Within a few weeks I was taking drugs regularly. Daniel and I would go over to Jody and Phil's and we'd all take them together. Daniel liked the effects as much as I did. At the beginning it was purely social, but soon I was taking them more often. Every few days, when the girls were sleeping and Daniel was at work, I'd slip a small white pill into my mouth. The effects were dramatic. I had loads of energy, felt confident and strong, stayed awake for ages and, best of all, as far as I was concerned, I had no appetite.

I had been a size sixteen all through my early teens. After I had Emily I went down to a size fourteen, and after Sophie I lost a bit more. But once I started taking the drugs the weight just fell off me, and before I knew it I was a size ten. Suddenly I could wear the pretty clothes other girls wore. I wasn't the dumpy one, hiding in a baggy jumper; I could slip into a mini-skirt or a cropped top and feel good. I used to look at myself in the mirror and think, is that really me? Tanya was the pretty, slim one in our family, and I'd always felt like the ugly one. That went very deep – all the years of name-calling and hurtful comments, mainly from Mum, had made me feel so bad about myself that it wasn't easy to change. I still felt ugly, but at least I was slim and ugly, and that did help my confidence.

To my delight, I was able to slip into the gorgeous size-ten white wedding dress Jody had got from her sister. Daniel and I got married when I was just nineteen and he was twenty-three.

It was a quiet wedding, but lovely. We were able to pay for it after I was awarded £7,500 in compensation for the abuse I had suffered at the hands of Terry and George. It was some-thing Anna had fought for over the years – she was deter-mined both Tanya and I should have it, after what we had been through – and I was so grateful to her when it finally came through. I hadn't really believed it would ever happen. It was a huge sum to us. After we had paid £1,000 for the wedding and honeymoon, we saved the rest, handing £2,000 to Daniel's dad to invest for us. He already had some shares, and he put our money into them too, all in his name. That left us with £4,500, which we put into the bank.

Emily was almost three and Sophie was a few months old when we married. They were our guests of honour, wearing pretty little mint coloured bridesmaid's dresses. All of Daniel's family came and, on my side, Dad and Sandra and Nan. I didn't know where Paul was, Tanya wasn't speaking to me, Jamie was still convalescing and I didn't invite Mum because I knew she'd find a way to spoil it for me, and I wasn't going to let anything – or anyone – do that.

We married in the local register office and had a buffet reception in the local social club. Then Daniel and I had a week-long honeymoon in Turkey, while his parents looked after the girls. It was the first time Daniel or I had ever been on a plane or travelled abroad. We sat side by side, amazed that this huge metal thing could lift off the ground, and both of us were relieved when it landed safely. We had a brilliant week, lying on the beach, playing in the sea and wandering in the local village, fascinated by all the foods and trinkets and clothes we'd never seen before.

Once we were back at home, everything seemed a bit flat. So I started going out on Friday nights with Daniel's sister, Joanne, who by this time was training to be an accountant. We went out to local pubs and clubs and had a really good time. Soon we were going out on Fridays and Saturdays, and then Sundays too. Daniel said he didn't mind. Looking back, he probably did, but I think he felt it wouldn't be fair to ask me to stay in all the time. He didn't really want to go out, and we couldn't afford a babysitter anyway, so he looked after the girls while I let my hair down and danced and drank with his sister.

All I wanted was some fun. It was so good to get out of the house and to feel like more than just a mum. And once I was dressed up and out partying, I found I was getting a lot of attention from men. That was new. In the past I was never noticed, but now I'd lost weight and dyed my hair much blonder, lots of men offered me drinks, asked for my number and wanted to go out with me. I always said no – I didn't want to cheat on Daniel, I just wanted to have a good time and feel young. But I couldn't help being flattered by all the attention I was getting. And when I was home with Daniel again, it was hard not to see him as a bit dull. I tried to get him to go out with me, but he wouldn't. 'You go on, I'll be fine at home,' he'd say, giving me a peck on the cheek.

Our life had settled into a steady routine. He would come home at half past six and I'd have tea ready. Then he'd relax with a few cans of lager while I bathed the girls and put them to bed. And by ten we'd go to bed too. I couldn't help feeling that Daniel was old before his time, and I didn't want to be like that, I wanted to enjoy being young while I had the chance.

One day, a couple of months after my wedding, I bumped into Tanya in the street. She did a double-take. 'God, Louise, I'd heard you'd lost weight, but you look amazing,' she said.

'Thanks,' I said. 'How are you?' Then I realised she was pregnant.

'Congratulations,' I said. 'I bet Gary's happy about it.'

'I'm not with Gary any more,' she said. 'We split and I'm with Gerald now – the baby's his. I'm not working, just looking after Callum and waiting for the baby. Why don't you come over and see me later?'

I was startled. Was this Tanya thawing out and wanting to be friends again? If so, then I was happy. 'OK,' I said. 'But I'm not sure where you're living.'

I knew she had moved in with Cheryl a few months earlier. Cheryl had a house on a brand new estate up the road, but some of the people on her street had found out that she was on the game and gone round and smashed her windows in. It must have been really frightening for her, alone there with her little son, and she probably welcomed Tanya's company. But if Tanya had split with Cheryl's brother, perhaps she had moved out?

'I'm still at Cheryl's,' she said. 'I look after the kids while she's at work. Gerald doesn't live with me, he's got his own place up the road. He shares with some mates and I don't want to live there – his friends are too wild. So Gerald comes to see me at my place.'

It was all a lot to take in. Tanya pregnant, by some guy I'd never met. And from what she said, they weren't likely to stay together. He sounded like someone who didn't want the commitment. And Tanya must know it.

'I'll come round at tea time,' I told her. 'I'll bring the girls.'

I did, and Tanya and I became friends again. I was glad. I'd worried about her and wanted to be there for her. And I'd missed her.

That summer she had a little girl, Michelle. And, to no-one's surprise, her boyfriend disappeared. So Tanya decided to go back to Pete, the father of her first baby.

And in September I decided to leave Daniel. We had only been married for seven months. I knew he'd be devastated, and his family too. I knew I wasn't being fair to him. But I felt I had to do it. I was fond of Daniel, but I didn't really love him. He'd always been good to me, and had loved me when I was fat and no-one else looked at me. He had stood by me and was the father of my girls. He was a good person. But I was beginning to feel as if my life was over before it had started. And I wanted to go out and live.

Chapter Seventeen

Daniel was very bitter about me leaving him. He didn't want the marriage to end, and he couldn't understand how I could do it. The way he saw it, we'd had everything, and I'd thrown it away.

I could see why he felt the way he did. But for me it was different. I had been with him since I was fourteen and I felt hemmed in. Losing so much weight and then finding that other men were attracted to me opened up a whole new world, and I wanted to be out there in it.

I felt so sorry and so guilty for hurting Daniel. If there had been a way I could have done it without causing him pain, I would have. As it was, his hurt became bitterness and anger, which made him want to hurt me.

The house was in my name, as I'd signed the council documents, so Daniel moved back in with his parents. He took everything he could – including the TV, stereo and PlayStation. Then he froze our bank account, so that I couldn't get hold of the money we had put away, from my compensation. He told me I would never have it. He had the phone cut off – we had one by then – because it was in his name.

The phone and the TV I could cope with, but I didn't know what to do about the money. That money meant such a lot to me, because it was an acknowledgment of the pain and suffering I had been through. I couldn't bear the thought of losing it. In the end, Daniel let me have £2,000, but he took the other £4,500, including the money we had given to his father to invest. His parents were devastated by the split; they blamed me, and supported Daniel in keeping the money. They told me I would have to prove that it was mine. And just to rub it in, Daniel spent some of it on things for his mum's house, including a giant TV and a stereo.

There was nothing I could do, but it was a bitter pill to swallow. And I wasn't wise with the money I did have. It disappeared in a matter of weeks – spent on drugs, nights out and gifts for the kids. I should have put some by, but I didn't. I felt heady with my new freedom and by this time I was experimenting with more drugs. I had tried both cocaine and ecstasy, though mostly I still just took amphetamines.

After the money was gone, I had to survive on benefits, because Daniel refused to give me any money. I couldn't go out to work, because the girls were still only two and four. It was tough, and of course there was no money for drugs or to pay babysitters so that I could go out.

Daniel also refused to have the girls regularly. At first he didn't see them at all, saying that he needed time to get his head round the split. Then he saw them, but refused to have them overnight, saying there wasn't room at his mum's. He was determined not to give me a break, and did everything he could to make my life difficult.

It wasn't long before I met a new man. Trevor was out clubbing with some mates one night when he caught my eye and then came over and offered to buy me a drink. We started seeing one another, and within weeks I was head over heels in love. It made me even more certain that I hadn't really loved Daniel. He'd offered me security, which I had needed so badly, and for that I would always be grateful, but I wanted to love someone, and I thought I'd found my ideal man in Trevor. He was twenty-five, tall and skinny, with large eyes. He didn't move in with me because he had his own house a few streets away from mine. He used to come over at night, once the girls were in bed, so he didn't have much to do with them. I hoped things might get more serious between us, but after we'd been together for almost a year, a local kid told me they had seen Trevor's car parked outside the house of a girl I thought was a really close friend on Christmas Day.

He was having an affair with her and I was devastated. We had a huge row, and he denied it at first, before admitting it and saying he didn't really love me anyway. I felt doubly betrayed, and all my old feelings of not being good enough surfaced with a vengeance.

For days I just cried. I had thought I'd met the perfect man, and he turned out to be just another two-timing creep. I felt so low for a while that I thought of killing myself. But I couldn't leave my girls. They were beautiful, and I knew I had to stay around to protect and love them.

I decided to move house, and went into a private rental, in the same street as Tanya. The house wasn't in a great state – it smelled of damp and looked tatty – but I felt I needed a change, so I took it. My rent was paid for me, as I was on benefits. I had thought a new house would give me a fresh start, but I still felt very low.

Once I'd moved in, I realised the house was in a worse state than I'd thought. There were mushrooms growing out of the dining room wall, and the kitchen ceiling was caving in. It was so damp that the kitchen lights didn't work. A friend advised me to call the council's environmental health department. They came round and discovered, among other things, that the living-room fire was emitting poisonous carbon monoxide – it could have killed me and the girls.

I called the landlord and asked him to fix some of the problems. He arrived with his two heavyweight, menacing sons and began threatening me. One of his sons pushed me up against a wall and told me I'd better get out and stop causing trouble. Then he kissed me on the cheek, in a really spine-chilling way, and told me he'd be back. I was terrified. I went round to the council's housing office and begged for somewhere new to live, but they told me I'd have to wait months.

I couldn't afford to get the repairs done myself, so I had to live, with my girls, in a damp, dangerous house, with a boarded-up window and a fire we couldn't use.

By this time Daniel had met a girl called Lisa, who was from South Africa. They got a house together, only a few streets from me. Daniel knew what a difficult time I was having and how little money I had, but he refused to help me. Even though he was now happy with Lisa, he remained angry and bitter.

He asked me for a divorce and told me that the only way we could avoid a £250 fee each was if I admitted to having an affair. This wasn't true, of course, but I believed what he said and decided to agree, to keep things simple and avoid the costs. There was no way I could have found that kind of money. We got the divorce, and then he said that one day he would show the girls my admission of an affair and tell them I had ruined his life.

I was devastated. I had always trusted Daniel. But he had changed. He had tricked me and was planning to tell our daughters I'd had an affair, when he knew it wasn't true. I could only hope and pray that he didn't really mean it, and that if he did, the girls would believe me.

Soon after this, Daniel came round to tell me he was going to South Africa to marry Lisa. He said, 'I'll have a better life over there.'

'What about the girls?' I asked, shocked that he could think of leaving them. He looked uncomfortable. 'I'll write,' he said. 'And they can come and see me when they're older.'

He left a couple of weeks later, leaving me to bring up our daughters alone. For the next few years he had almost no contact with the girls, apart from a few phone calls, and he paid no maintenance.

The person who did come through for us was his mother, Rose. She had been very angry with me after the split, but she didn't stay angry. We made up and became good friends. And she started having the girls over once a month for the weekend. I felt glad that even though they couldn't see their dad, they could at least be part of his family.

After Daniel left, I was so broke that I started looking after Tanya's three children for her, while she was at work. She had gone back on the game after Michelle was born. Then she'd got pregnant again, by Pete, and had another son. When he was a few weeks old she went back to work again, three days a week. Now she was raking in money – she could make between two and three hundred pounds a day. I couldn't believe how much cash she seemed to have. She was forever buying clothes and fancy haircuts, as well as nice things for her house and kids, while I had nothing.

Tanya worked during the day and was supposed to finish at six. But she often didn't arrive to pick up the kids until eight, and sometimes she'd stay away all night, without calling me to tell me where she was. She had split with Pete again, and she had loads of boyfriends and a hectic social life, and would just take off with one of them. Despite this, she only paid me £20 a day, for all three children. It was exhausting looking after five of them for hour after hour, especially for so little. I used to feel very jealous of Tanya.

I began to think about how good it would be to have that kind of money myself. I could sort the house out, get things for the girls, have nice clothes and give us a good life. Could I do what Tanya was doing? I didn't know. I wasn't at all sure whether I could get that kind of work – or whether I could go through with it.

I told Tanya I was thinking about it. She had always said it was so easy, and that many of the men she saw didn't even want sex, they just wanted someone to talk to. But when I suggested that I might do it she told me I wouldn't have the bottle.

That was what decided me. She thought I was too scared, that I couldn't pull it off. Well, I'd show her. And Mum too.

I was seeing Mum from time to time, and I knew she was proud of what Tanya was doing – mainly because Tanya often gave her money or paid for her nights out. But she didn't think I could do it – she told me I didn't have the guts. Mum's catchphrase was 'Why give it when you can sell it?' She was always saying it. I began to think that maybe she was right. I didn't have any skills or qualifications. My body was the one thing I had that might be worth something.

Once I'd made up my mind, Tanya decided to help me. She worked for a man who ran two houses, in different parts of the city, and she arranged for me to have an 'interview' at one of them. She told me what to wear and what would happen and although I felt sick with apprehension, I wasn't going to let myself back out. I took some speed to help with my nerves, and then dressed as though I was going out for a Saturday night on the town – full make-up, short skirt and sexy underwear.

The house I was told to go to was in a rundown area of town. I walked past the terraced houses – most of which looked as though they had seen better days, some boarded up – feeling glad I didn't have to live there.

I rang the bell and stood on the doorstep, trying to calm my nerves and wondering what on earth I was doing. Reggie opened the door and told me to come in. He was a sallow, middle-aged man, with dark, slightly greasy hair and a smarmy smile.

I was surprised to find that the house itself was decorated really nicely, with fresh paint and new furnishings. It looked clean and welcoming, and was a total contrast to the rundown exterior.

As I stood in the hallway, looking around me, Reggie beckoned me up the stairs. My stomach turned over. For a moment I had forgotten the interview. He led me into a pleasantly furnished bedroom and told me, in a very matter of fact manner, to undress and rub him down. 'I want a massage and an oral,' he said, pointing to a bag of condoms at the side of the bed.

I felt sick and my hands shook as I slowly began to undress. I tried to blank out what was happening, just as I had with George and Terry. All I could think about was getting it over with as soon as possible. I had goosebumps on my arms as I climbed onto the bed where Reggie was lying, naked, on his stomach. He turned his head and eyed me in a strategically placed mirror.

'Don't bother with the oil,' he said, as I reached tentatively for the bottle. Obediently I put it down and began to massage him. The next twenty minutes seemed to last forever. I tried not to look up at the clock, but I couldn't help sneaking a peek at it now and then, praying that time would go quicker. Then Reggie turned over and told me to perform the oral. I thought about running out of the room, crying, screaming, anything to stop what was happening. I felt panicky and tearful but, struggling not to show it, I did as he asked.

When it was over, he jumped off the bed and dropped the condom in a bin. 'You'll do,' he said, looking at me. 'You can start tomorrow. But from now on you provide your own condoms – your Tanya will show where you can get them for nowt.'

I pulled on my clothes as fast as I could and followed him out of the room and back down the stairs. 'You get £40 per customer,' he said. 'You give £15 to me, and the rest is yours.' I nodded and mumbled my thanks as I bolted out of the door.

Outside, I brushed away my tears as I headed back to the bus stop. I'd done it, but I didn't know whether to be pleased or sad, ashamed or proud. Was this really what I wanted to do? I felt like running back and telling him it had all been a mistake. But I thought of the money and how badly I needed it, and got on the bus.

The next day I dressed up again, in a little mini-skirt, boots and a tight top, dropped the kids off with Mum, who'd agreed to look after them, and went back to the house. He'd told me to report at ten a.m., though I couldn't imagine men queuing up for sex at that hour. Surely they'd all want to come later in the day?

I was wrong. From the minute I got there, the place was busy. I was one of two girls working that day, and neither of us got much of a break. Goodness knows what the neighbours thought. They must have guessed what was going on, with so many men coming and going, but I was told that they didn't complain.

Punters would ring up – the number was advertised all over town and the phone rang constantly – and Reggie would ask what kind of girl they wanted and describe whoever he thought would fit the bill. I listened to him describing me – an attractive blonde, nineteen years old, big blue eyes, size ten, 34b chest, with a pert bum. Then he'd give them details of where the house was, opening times and prices.

When clients arrived to see me, I had to greet them and

take them upstairs. Reggie had a little monitor next to his chair in the downstairs office, so that he could hear what was happening upstairs. He claimed this was for my safety, but I wasn't too sure about that. I reckoned he was just a dirty old man who liked listening.

It was the hardest day's work I had ever done. But I was good at numbing myself to get through it, and none of the customers demanded anything bizarre or scary. I saw thirteen men that day, but I only had sex with five of them. A couple ejaculated before I'd even touched them, and the rest just wanted the massage, or to talk.

When I finished work at six, I went home with £325. I kept opening my bag to look at it. I couldn't believe I'd made more than most people I knew earned in a week. But it had been hard-earned. I went home, sat in the bath and scrubbed myself for half an hour and tried to forget where I had been and what I'd done.

After my second day at work, I was able to buy us a washing machine and a tumble dryer. I was so proud of myself. I blanked out what I'd done to earn them, telling myself it was the only way we could survive.

From then on I worked two days a week. The customers were very similar to those I saw on my first day – some wanted straight sex, some just a massage or oral sex, and some just wanted to talk or watch me undress.

Most weeks I took home over £500 for fifteen hours work

– and it was tax free. I had never before had that kind of money. I bought things for the house, for the kids and for myself. I splashed out on a new TV, furniture, toys and clothes. But the money came at a higher and higher price. I spent a lot of it on drugs, because taking them helped me to blot out what I was doing to myself.

The more I earned, the more I partied, taking more and more drugs and going out three or four times a week. I spent the money as quick as I earned it and never thought of saving any. And I'd started drinking a lot more. Sometimes I'd binge and get really drunk, downing shots and spirits as though they were water. Of course, I'd wake up with a terrible hangover. But then I'd take more drugs, to get high again.

Inevitably, with all this going on, I wasn't being a great mum. I adored my girls, but I was spending a lot less time with them. Instead of being with them, as I had before, I was buying their affection with toys, PlayStations, games, clothes, TVs and videos. I didn't stop to think that all this was no substitute for time with their mum.

My own mum was delighted with my new job, because I was paying her to look after the girls. She was earning from both me and Tanya, and she loved it. She was still living with Alan, though they'd never married because she couldn't track down Craig to divorce him. She looked after all five of our kids in the same flat I'd lived in with her, next to the pub. I'd had doubts about letting her look after my girls – she'd been a pretty awful mother and I didn't want her mistreating the girls. But I needed someone to look after them, and she was there. And I suppose I hoped she would be different with them and make up for what a rotten mother she'd been.

She wasn't drinking, which I took as a good sign. But my hopes that she'd mellowed were dashed when the girls began telling me that they were scared of her. It seemed she was losing her temper and shouting at them and they spent most of their time trying not to spark her off. When I realised this, I was horrified. How could I have thought she would change?

Within a couple of days, I had found a new childminder, a girl called Alison, who lived up the road. She was blonde, plump and cheerful, and was on her own with her little boy. She was on the game too, so she looked after my two when I was working and I looked after her little boy when she was at work. The girls settled with her and were much happier and I liked her too. We became good friends, and started going on nights out together.

I soon got friendly with some of the other girls who were working in the same house. Tanya worked at the other one, and in time I got to know the girls there too, through her. We'd all chat between customers and we started going out on the town together after work. They were a nice bunch, all of them trying to make ends meet, just like me and Tanya. And for me, getting to know them was the best thing about the job. I loved having a new set of friends. I felt easy with them, because we all did the same thing, so there was no need to pretend. We gossiped about punters, sympathised with one another, helped each other out and had wild nights on the town.

I'd been there for a few months when Tanya started to get jealous because I was doing better than she was. I was the new girl, and that seemed to attract lots of the clients. Tanya decided to tell Reggie I was taking drugs. He was furious, even though I wasn't taking them at work. He didn't want the girls becoming junkies, so he gave me a warning and told me not to come in for a week. Tanya took my shifts and earned double money that week. I was annoyed with her, but I knew I wasn't supposed to be taking drugs, so I had to accept my punishment.

I thought Tanya wouldn't do it again, but when I took drugs the following weekend, she told Reggie. This time he sacked me.

I decided that perhaps the job wasn't for me. Although I liked the money and the other girls, I hated the rest of it. I decided I would find an ordinary job – one which paid less, but would leave my dignity and pride intact. The problem was that I couldn't stop spending money. I was used to having it and to being able to buy all kinds of things. And of course I still wanted drugs. So I kept spending, and the debts soon started piling up.

Within weeks, I was desperate for money and knee-deep in bills. And I only knew one way to get them paid.

I called up a woman I'd heard about through one of the other girls. She ran a house in the centre of town – a nice place, I was told – where the money was good. I went for an interview – a real one this time – and she told me I could start the following week.

Chapter Eighteen

The new massage parlour was a lot smarter than the old one. Outside, it just looked like any respectable home. Inside, it was all white and clean and professional, with dark-wood furnishings and beautiful potted plants. There were two bedrooms, each with a mirrored wall and a big double bed in the middle of the room, with lovely burgundy sheets and pillows.

The hours were longer – I had to work from ten in the morning until ten at night, but the atmosphere was more relaxed because there was no boss on the premises. Two of us girls worked each day, and we did everything, including answering the phones, taking bookings and totting up the takings, which were also better than at my last place. Here we charged between £50 and £60 for half an hour, and £10 of that went to the boss, who came in the evening to collect the money and lock up.

Tanya was still at the old place, and she was very jealous that I was somewhere classier, making more money. Our relationship had been strained since she lost me my last job, and now it became worse.

Then I heard that Mum had split up with Alan. I was sorry, because they'd been together a few years and he was so much nicer than most of her other men. But I guessed that in the end he'd had enough. Mum and Tanya had started going out together, picking up men. Tanya attracted all sorts of men, and Mum took the opportunity to get in on the action. I was disgusted, and didn't want anything to do with it, so I seldom saw either of them.

I worked two days a week for the next few months and gradually built up a clientele of regulars. Most of the men who came there were successful, married men with plenty of money, who just wanted straight sex. But there were a few horrible, scruffy types who saved up to come every few months, and I dreaded them. I coped by switching off, and going onto autopilot.

Then there were the odd ones, with weird fetishes and fantasies. Many of them were harmless, eccentric and a bit sad. None of them seemed to me to be remotely sexy. There was one we called 'jelly baby man'. He looked so ordinary – medium height, pleasant face, in his mid-forties. The first time I saw him I thought he was just an average Joe. But then we got to the bedroom and he pulled out a packet of jelly babies and told me what he wanted. I tried hard to keep a straight face as he asked to lie on the bed, naked and face down, while I, fully dressed, put the jelly babies all over his arms, legs, back and shoulders. Next I had to slowly pick them off him, with my mouth, and eat them, while telling him what I was doing. Before I'd eaten them all he would have climaxed and it would all be over. He would get dressed, pay me and leave. He visited about once a week – luckily, I quite liked jelly babies.

Another guy was known as 'shoe man'. He looked a bit like Elton John, and all he wanted was for me to stand, dressed, sideways-on to the mirrored wall, wearing my highest stiletto heels. He would get undressed and kneel in front of me, looking at my shoes. Then he would begin to touch, kiss and lick them, before ejaculating on them. We would only have been in the room for ten minutes by the time he paid me and left. I found his behaviour so bizarre, but I knew from my own experience, as well as what the other girls told me, that there were plenty of men with similar fetishes.

Another regular was 'doggy man'. He loved to have me put a dog collar around his neck and walk him – on all fours and stark naked – up and down the bedroom and then into the waiting room in front of other customers and the girls. As I walked him, he would bark loudly and I would tell him he was a good doggy. Of course everyone who saw him laughed, but humiliation was what he liked – he would often ask me to whip him and tell him he had been a naughty doggy.

Strangest of all was the one we called 'baby man', who would arrive late in the evening, with a bag in his hand. I'd heard the other girls laughing about him, but the first time I met him I didn't realise who he was. Coming to the end of a busy shift and thinking he was just another ordinary client, I asked him to go ahead and wait for me in the bedroom.

When I opened the door, a few minutes later, I did a double-take. He was perched on the edge of the bed, naked, with a very large nappy next to him. While I did my best not to look surprised or amused, he asked me if I knew what he wanted me to do. I did, from the other girls' descriptions, so I nodded.

I had to lie him on the bed and put the nappy on him. Then he sat up on the edge of the bed and put a dummy in his mouth, before sitting on my knee, where I had to rock him back and forth as he gurgled with joy. Then I had to 'wind' him and tell him he was a good boy, as he mumbled 'Mummy' back to me. And that was it. He didn't even appear to be sexually aroused. After about ten minutes, he got up, thanked me, got back into his business suit, paid me and slipped out of the house, back into the busy city, thronging with commuters, all totally unaware of his secret.

Afterwards, I could barely believe what had happened. Why would an adult man want to pretend to be a baby? A shrink would probably say that he was trying to make up for something he missed out on as a child, but we girls just found him plain odd.

After twelve hours of seeing clients, I would go home, exhausted, have a hot bath and fall into bed.

Some weeks I was making as much as £1000, but I would

always blow the lot on going out, clothes, drugs and stuff for the kids. I never saved a penny. I began going out on the town two or three nights a week with Alison. We'd become best friends. I had never really had a close girlfriend before; it was good to have someone to talk to and go out with.

I loved being out in the clubs around town. I was slim and blonde and had lots of nice clothes, so I got plenty of attention from men. I loved it when they told me I was gorgeous – probably because deep down I never really believed it. I still saw myself as the plump, unattractive kid.

Alison and I took a lot of drugs together. She was as bad as I was, and sometimes worse. We encouraged one another, avoiding having to think about our working lives by getting off our heads, first on alcohol and then on amphetamines and ecstasy. We were taking terrible risks, but we didn't see it that way – we just thought we were having fun.

One night I was in a club when a good-looking boy came over and started chatting me up. He told me his name was Neil, and asked if I knew where he could get some pills. I did, and he was impressed. He asked for my number and I gave it to him – I thought he was gorgeous. The next day he called me and we went out on a date. We laughed all night – I was in love again.

It wasn't long before Neil moved in with me. I was being just like my mum; I had to have a man around to make me feel secure. The funny thing was that the men I got involved with never did make me feel secure. My last boyfriend had flirted with other girls and went off with my friend, and Neil was unemployed and happy to live off my earnings from the massage parlour. At the time I didn't think it mattered. My sense of self-worth was non-existent; I was grateful if anyone wanted to be with me, even if I had to buy their company. I just thought that, as I had plenty of money, it was OK if Neil didn't work. And I closed my eyes to his laziness and selfishness. He didn't really care about me, but then I had no idea what it was really like to be cared for by someone else. I thought the best I could ever hope for was someone who was prepared to stick around, even if they spent most of their day with their feet up, watching my TV.

One evening I came home from work to find the front door ajar. Neil was out with some mates, and the girls were with my mum, so I knew the house was empty. The door should have been locked. I looked at the lock and saw it was broken. Someone had forced it.

Feeling very scared, I pushed the door open and waited a moment. There was silence. I was pretty sure that whoever had been in had gone, but I was still very, very nervous as I stepped inside and switched the light on. I called out, but there was no answer. I peered into the front room – and gasped. The room was almost bare. The TV was gone, along with my music centre and all my CDs. So were my ornaments, a couple of the chairs, the rug and the pictures off the walls. By the time I got upstairs and saw that all my things and the kids' things had gone, I was in tears. Most of my clothes and jewellery, the girls' PlayStation and TV and even their toys were gone. Who could have done this to us?

I wasn't insured. I called the police and a couple of officers came round, but they told me I'd be very lucky to get any of it back. My stuff would have been sold on within hours, and finding the thieves would be like looking for a needle in a haystack.

After the police had gone, I sat on the sofa – which was just about all that was left in the front room – and waited for Neil. I was in a daze, shocked to have lost almost everything I had and scared that whoever did it would come back for the rest. I couldn't believe that I'd had sex with all those men for nothing – everything I'd bought with my hard-earned money had gone. I felt physically sick.

When Neil finally came in, a couple of hours later, I told him what had happened. He'd had a few drinks and stank of booze, and he didn't seem too worried. 'Never mind,' he said, 'you make enough money, you can always buy it all again.'

That hurt. I worked hard for my money, and it would take a long time to replace everything. He didn't seem to care about how upset I was. Lying in bed that night, I decided we had to get out, as soon as possible. We were already under notice to leave, but I hadn't yet done anything about finding us somewhere new. Now I had to – and fast.

I felt so low that night. Neil was snoring beside me. He

didn't seem bothered by what had happened, but it had shaken me. Why did so many bad things happen to me? Had I been born with an unlucky streak? Had I done something to deserve all the misery and trouble that seemed to dog me? I tried so hard to be nice to people, to look after my girls, to do the right thing. Yet somehow things always went wrong. I wondered if it would ever change.

The next morning I went to see the local council housing manager and explained the situation. She looked doubtful. 'I'll see what I can do,' she said. 'But there aren't a lot of properties available, so don't raise your hopes about getting somewhere nice.'

I knew we had a high chance of ending up on a really rough estate. So when the council letter arrived two weeks later, I was scared to open it. Whatever they offered we would have to take – we were running out of time.

When I read the letter I screamed with joy. We'd been offered a house in a really nice area. I skipped around the kitchen and the girls, seeing how excited I was, tried to join in. 'We've got a new home, girls,' I said. 'We'll be safe there and there will be a nice school for you nearby.'

'Ooh, Mummy, no more robbers,' Emily said. She had been inconsolable when her toys were taken, and still wasn't sleeping well.

'No more robbers,' I grinned. 'We'll get you some more toys and this time nobody will take them.'

For the next few weeks I saved up all my money. We more or less camped in the house, because I didn't replace anything. The front door wouldn't lock and several times I got home to find someone had been in and more of our things – the precious few we had left – had been taken.

By the time we moved into our new house we had almost nothing left to take with us. But I'd stopped caring. I just wanted to be out of that awful house and make a new start. The new place was nice – three bedrooms, a garden and a decent neighbourhood. I got busy painting and decorating it and the first things I bought were some lovely bedroom furniture and new toys for the girls.

Things seemed to be looking up. I decided it was time I learned to drive and I loved it. In a few weeks I passed my test and bought a little second-hand car. I couldn't believe the feeling of freedom it gave me! No more hanging around at bus stops, lugging shopping and the girls' things. I could just pile all of us into the car and go.

Emily started at the local school and settled in straight away, while Sophie was looked after by a local childminder on weekdays, and Alison had both girls on Saturdays. Everything seemed to be coming together. But it wasn't, because despite all the good things, there was a dark shadow hanging over us – a drug-induced shadow.

Neil had always used drugs, but by this time he was using every day. And he had begun dealing. When I realised what he was doing, I became very worried and begged him to stop, but he refused. 'It's just a little bit,' he said. 'What's the problem?'

So I tried to turn a blind eye to it. And the best way to do that was to take drugs myself. I began taking more and more amphetamines and ecstasy. When I was high everything seemed good, there were no problems and all I wanted to do was party. But when I came down again the next day, it all hit me – I was on the game, my boyfriend was selling drugs, our lives were a mess. I couldn't deal with it, so I took more drugs, to blot it all out. I was spending every weekend high and topping up during the week too.

Worst of all, I was letting my kids down, and I knew it. I wanted to be the best mum in the world, and I couldn't. I did my best to be there for them, and I didn't take drugs around them, but I was only capable of being half there while I was living that way.

I refused to face it, because it hurt too much. Instead I just took more drugs. They killed my appetite, so the weight fell off me. I was down to a size six – so skinny that everyone who knew me was worried. Even Mum and Tanya, on the rare occasions when I saw them, had started to nag me about the drugs and the state of my health.

Neil was changing too. The drugs were making him aggressive and violent. Several times he attacked me, pinning me against the wall and threatening to really hurt me. I was scared of him and didn't know what to do. He was always asking me for money, but at the same time he kept badgering me to give up working in the massage parlour and get another job. I decided I would. The job I was doing was soul-destroying; it had stopped being worth the money.

We had a friend who said she might be able to get me a job in the clothes shop where she worked. A week later she told me I had an interview. I dressed smartly, made sure I wasn't high, and got the job, working eleven to three, five days a week. This was it – my new start. Except that it wasn't, because I was still taking drugs. I began calling in sick so often that I was soon in danger of getting the sack.

My life was falling apart. I could barely hold down my job, and with a lot less money coming in, I was broke. I was taking drugs and ruining my health. I was sending my kids to babysitters when I should have been there for them myself. And my relationship was miserable.

Neil was becoming more and more paranoid and jealous. He kept accusing me of seeing other men and checking for evidence. When he came in he would look in the ashtrays to see if there was an unfamiliar cigarette butt there. Of course there wasn't, because I wasn't seeing anyone else. But he wouldn't believe it.

Then one day he let slip something that shook me badly. He had been behind the robbery in our last house. He had told the thieves, friends of his, when we would be out, so that they could kick the door in – and he'd taken a cut of the money they made. I stared at him, too shocked to speak. 'What's the problem?' he drawled, a sick smile on his face. 'Nobody got hurt.'

'I did,' I said. 'The girls did. You betrayed us.' Suddenly I saw him clearly. A rat who would sell us out for drug money.

'Get out,' I told him. 'Get out and don't come back.' I was shaking. I knew he might turn on me, but I was so angry I didn't care. When I realised Neil had robbed me, something in me snapped. I'd had enough – of him, of the way we were living, of drugs, and of being used.

Neil packed a bag and left that night. 'I'm not bothered,' he spat over his shoulder as he went out of the door. 'I'm seeing someone else anyway.'

I didn't care. She was welcome to him. It was just me and my girls now, and I was going to be there for them and give them the life they deserved. I had no idea how – but I knew I had to find a way.

Chapter Nineteen

For a couple of months, I carried on taking drugs. Then I realised that if things were really going to change, I had to stop.

It was harder than I thought.

Coming off drugs meant getting past my body's craving for them. I was so used to being high that staying clean felt weird and flat. I paced around, drank endless cups of tea and smoked a lot. I tried to eat, but I had no appetite. I couldn't sleep and I couldn't concentrate on anything. I stared at the TV without seeing what was on and had to summon up all my energy to manage the girls.

A couple of times I slipped up, when friends urged me to take drugs. I realised I was going to have to change everything – including my friends. That was hard. I was still seeing Alison several times a week. But she was taking drugs every day, even when her small son was around. She laughed when I said I wanted to stop. So I began to cool off, making excuses not to go out, and I found another childminder. I still saw her – she would have the kids for me on Saturdays when Daniel's mum didn't have them – but I didn't spend time with her the way

I used to. It was really hard, because she meant a lot to me and I missed her. But I knew that if I was going to make it, I couldn't be with people who were still taking drugs.

Instead of going out two or three nights a week, I cut back to just once a fortnight. I spent a lot more time with the girls, and I became more reliable at work, turning up regularly and on time.

I didn't defeat all my demons at once. It was a hard slog. I was still working in the massage parlour on Saturdays, because my wage in the clothes shop just wasn't enough to live on. And I did relapse and take drugs occasionally. But I was determined that I was going to stop completely, and every time I let myself down by taking them again, I vowed to try even harder. It was just a matter of time.

After Neil had been gone for four months, my life was beginning to feel very different. So when Alison asked me to go out with her one evening I said yes. I hadn't been out with her for weeks, but I decided I felt strong enough to say no if drugs were around. I just wanted to let my hair down and have some fun.

It was just after Valentine's Day, in 2004. We went to a couple of bars and then one of the town's noisiest nightclubs, where we had a couple of drinks and a dance. I was laughing with Alison over a bit of gossip when I looked across the dance floor and saw a really fit-looking guy. He was looking at me, and when he caught my eye, he made his way over and offered to buy me a drink. He said his name was Matthew, and when we'd got our drinks we went over to a quieter spot to talk.

From the start I knew this guy was different. He was educated, intelligent, sensitive, thoughtful and funny. He seemed to really like me, but I couldn't work out why. I didn't think I was his type at all.

At the end of the evening we exchanged phone numbers. On the way home I told Alison how much I'd liked him. I wasn't sure if he'd call me – we'd both had a few drinks and I thought he might change his mind in the cold light of day. But he didn't – he called me and asked me out to lunch.

We met a couple of days later, in a restaurant in town, and I liked him even more than I had the first time. I told him I had two daughters and worked in a clothes shop. He told me he worked in the housing department of the local council, finding homes for families in need. He also told me about his very happy, loving family. His parents were still married, his dad had been an accountant all his life, they'd always gone to church every Sunday and he had a brother and sister he loved very much.

When he told me his brother was a head teacher, I was amazed. Matthew came from a world that was so different from mine, I just didn't know if we could ever bridge the gap. He was a man with a serious, worthwhile job, from a good background. What would he think if he knew the truth about me?

We began seeing each other regularly. Matthew was so caring and interested in me that in many ways it felt strange. I'd never been around a man like that before. I was used to being ignored, used and put down. Now here was someone who gave me flowers and gifts and came over to walk me to work in the morning.

I should have been so happy, but instead I felt tortured. I was so afraid that if Matthew found out the truth about me, he would run a mile. Every time I saw him I thought about telling him, but I couldn't face it. I wanted to hang on to just a little joy and normality and happiness before I burst the bubble.

I thought about not telling him at all. But I knew it wasn't an option. It would have meant living with so many secrets. One day, somehow, he would learn the truth, and it would be worse if I had lied. Matthew was already asking to meet my family. What would he think of my mum, with her badly dyed hair, foul language and scarred arms? What would he think of my sister, who was still on the game? And, worst of all, what would he think of me, for becoming a prostitute and taking drugs?

Matthew wasn't a saint, I knew that. It wasn't that I put him on a pedestal. He was just a normal guy. But it made me realise – as if I didn't know already – just how far from normal my own upbringing had been.

I decided that I had to tell him the truth before he met the girls. I'd kept him away from them, because I didn't want to make it harder if we split up. I knew the girls would think he was great, and they'd been through enough already.

One day I decided I couldn't leave it any longer. We'd been seeing each other for a couple of months, and I felt it was getting serious. That was great – I wanted serious, but not until he knew the truth. That evening we went out and I made sure we both drank quite a bit. I knew I couldn't tell him if either of us was stone-cold sober.

Sitting in a wine bar, late in the evening, I told him some – not all – of my story. I owned up to being on the game – I had only given up Saturdays at the massage parlour after I met him – and to taking drugs.

Even cushioned by alcohol, he looked shocked. I could see it was hard for him to take it all in. After I'd told him, I said I was going home, to give him time to think. It was hard to walk away from him. I was afraid I'd never see him again. But I had to know if he would still want me now that he knew just how many mistakes I'd made.

I didn't sleep that night. Matthew always texted me in the mornings, so I kept my phone by my side, knowing that if everything was still OK I'd get a wake-up text.

When it came, I jumped. I'd dozed off, exhausted, frightened and sad. I grabbed my phone.

'Hi, babe,' it said. 'Are you OK after last night?'

I was relieved – but then the doubts set in. What if he didn't remember? He'd had a few drinks, perhaps he'd just blotted it out.

When I saw him again that evening I was sick with nerves. He seemed quite normal, but I was edgy, anxious and tense.

'You know,' he said, taking my hand, 'I remember everything. And it's OK. I love you and nothing's going to change that.'

That's when I cried. For all the hurt and desperation and rejection I had suffered. And for the love of this wonderful, forgiving man, who still wanted me.

After that we went from strength to strength. I took him home to meet the girls, and of course they adored him. He played with them, told me they were gorgeous and said he knew he'd love them as if they were his own.

He took me to meet his family, and I thought they were as lovely as he'd made them sound. His parents accepted me as one of the family straight away – along with my girls.

Everything seemed to be going so well that some mornings I had to pinch myself. I hadn't taken drugs since I'd met Matthew. Everything felt good, clean and new. I was being given another chance, and I was going to take it with both hands.

Then I missed a period.

I panicked. If I was pregnant would Matthew want to stay with me? We'd talked about children, but neither of us imagined it would be this soon. We hadn't even made plans to live together.

In a daze, I got a test. It was positive. I plucked up the courage to tell him that night. He looked at me incredulously – then he leaped up and hugged me.

'That's wonderful,' he said. 'Let's buy a house together. All I want is for you, me and the girls to be a family.'

'Me too,' I said, beaming.

The next few months weren't easy. It was a much rougher pregnancy than the first two, and I felt constantly sick. I had to give up work because I was missing so much. But despite this, we managed to buy a lovely house, with four bedrooms, in a nice area.

I had always told Matthew how much I regretted leaving school with no qualifications. He encouraged me to go to college, to do 'back to learning' courses in English and maths. I did them while I was pregnant, and I loved learning again. It made me feel that maybe I could make something of my life.

In the spring of 2005 I went into labour. At first everything seemed to be going well. Matthew came with me to the hospital while a friend looked after the girls. But after several hours in labour I was told that the baby was in distress and they needed to do an emergency caesarean. I was rushed into the operating theatre, with Matthew by my side.

The next thing I remember was coming round to see Matthew holding our little girl. 'She's gorgeous,' he said, as he put her into my arms. She was, and we called her Amy.

I was taken to the maternity ward and Amy was put into a cot beside me. A few hours later I drifted off to sleep, thinking how lucky I was to have another beautiful little girl.

That was the last thing I remember. In the following hours I became very ill. I had developed a serious infection and that night the doctors told Matthew that I might not survive.

I was a fighter – and I made it through the night and woke to find Matthew at my side. I was in intensive care, with needles and tubes sticking out of my feet and neck. It was two days before I could even talk. By then I had been moved to an ordinary ward, where I stayed for another nine days.

Thankfully, Rose looked after the older girls, while Matthew, who was on paternity leave, kept Amy with him. He looked after her on his own, changing her nappies, ringing his mum and asking her what he should do and then visiting me with her during the day.

I came home weak and tired and had to rest for the next few weeks. I was so grateful to have made it. After that, I wanted to be with the girls and Matthew as much as possible, just to appreciate what I had almost lost.

Emily and Sophie loved their little sister, and Matthew was wonderful. We'd moved home just before the birth, and in those weeks afterwards he looked after all of us and worked every spare hour decorating the girls' rooms first and then the rest of the house.

Three months later, I was back on my feet, grateful to be

alive and determined to make the most of all that I had. I wanted to get an education and a good job, but I didn't know where to start – or whether I could really do it.

One afternoon Matthew took me out in the car. 'Where are we going?' I asked him, but he wouldn't say. A few minutes later he pulled into the car park of the local further education college.

'Come on,' he said. 'You're always saying you want to study. Let's go in and sign you up.'

He was right, I was always saying it, and so far all I'd done was the back to learning courses. I went inside, feeling very nervous, and signed up to start GCSE courses in English and maths the following September. I was on my way!

Two months later I arrived for my first class. From the start I loved studying. It was as though a part of me had been starved and was now being fed. I lapped it up, did all my homework and couldn't wait for the next class. I liked the people I met there, and began to feel so much better about myself. I realised that I wasn't stupid; I could do the work and get good marks.

The following summer I passed both exams with flying colours. I had qualifications! It felt fantastic. By that time I was working in a local restaurant, doing a mixture of lunchtime and evening shifts, to fit in with Matthew and the girls. I really liked the job – my boss became a good friend and so did the other waitresses. I had a lovely childminder for Amy, and Emily and Sophie were happily settled in school.

Though I was in no rush to leave my job in the restaurant, I had a secret dream. I wanted to work with children in care. I knew what it felt like to be torn away from your family, and I felt I might be able to give them something. I decided to train as a teaching assistant, hoping that a qualification in working with children would help me towards my goal. A year later I passed those exams, and I began to feel that I really could do anything I wanted.

By that time I had told Matthew the full story of my childhood. It wasn't easy. I still felt a lot of shame and guilt about what had happened to me. Matthew was loving and accepting, and he helped me to understand – really understand – that none of it was my fault. I was let down and hurt by the adults around me, and all I could do was survive.

He suggested that we get hold of my social services files, so that I could fill in some of the missing parts of the story. It was surprisingly easy, but when I sat down to read them, I was stunned and deeply saddened. The files revealed that Mum had known all along that George and then Terry were abusing Tanya and me. She had known and had done nothing. I had always convinced myself that she hadn't realised and that her failure to help us had been through ignorance. But that wasn't true. She was more heartless and cruel than I could have imagined.

I was still seeing her from time to time. But after reading the files, I decided to stop having contact. I felt hurt and betrayed and knew I couldn't trust her again. I certainly didn't want my children to be around her. Tanya, who was still working as a prostitute, remained close to Mum, who looked after her three children. I hoped that Tanya and I could remain friends, but it was impossible. She refused to see the truth about Mum, and I couldn't hide from it. We had chosen such different paths that parting was inevitable.

As for Jamie and Paul, they both struggled to survive. Jamie was still living with his girlfriend, doing odd jobs and getting by. Paul had reappeared a few years back, but he had never managed to work and the last I heard of him he was hooked on heroin and sleeping on a mate's sofa.

I miss all of them ' especially Tanya, as we were once so close. But I know that losing my family was the price I had to pay for escaping my childhood demons and I wouldn't change anything. I have three beautiful daughters and a wonderful man by my side.

I still see Dad, though sadly Sandra died a couple of years ago. He's on his own now, and we get on well. He feels sad about the years he missed with me, and he loves seeing my girls and being a grandfather.

A few months ago, two wonderful things happened. First, Matthew came home and told me that a friend of his who worked in the council's education department was interested in offering me a part-time job as a mentor to children in care. I was thrilled – I knew I could give a lost and unhappy child love and support. I just wanted a chance to prove it. And I knew, too, that by helping other damaged children, I could heal some of the wounds from my own past.

The second thing that happened was even more wonderful. One evening Matthew took me out to dinner, then reached across the table and took my hand. 'Will you marry me?' he said softly. I looked at his warm, smiling face, and for a moment I couldn't speak. Was I really going to spend the rest of my life with this very special man?

'Yes,' I said. 'Oh yes. I will.'

Acknowledgements

This book would not have been possible without the belief, dedication, hard work and support of a number of special people.

Thank you to Judy Chilcote, my agent, who made me feel so at ease at our first meeting in London and who had the compassion to understand my story and believed in it from the start. Throughout my journey you have been wonderful.

Thank you to Caro Handley, my editor, who has been so caring and who gave me the courage and confidence to be able to put my past into words. You have been amazing to work with and I hope our paths cross again.

Thank you to Carly Cook at Headline Publishing for your kind words of support, your hard work in ensuring that we got everything done on time, and for adding the finishing touches that make my book special.

Finally a special thank you to my partner whose unconditional love has changed my life forever. There would be no story without you. You are and always will be my guardian angel. You were the very first person to believe in me and show me that 'I could', to help me understand my childhood and to move on. Without you to write my story we would never have gone on this journey together. I will always love you.

DESTROYED

JAYNE STERNE

When eight-year-old Jayne left bomb-torn Northern Ireland, her family stayed with relations and a distant relative began a campaign of abuse so horrifying that her world was shattered for ever.

And when the family moved again – her relative came too. Raped repeatedly, beaten, abused and battered, Jayne's life was a living hell.

One thing kept Jayne sane: the love and care of her older brother, Stuart. But he had demons of his own, and Jayne watched in despair as the boy who had always protected her turned into an adult consumed by rage. Out of control, Stuart went on to commit the 'Barbecue Murders', one of the most terrible crimes of recent years . . .

Destroyed is the heart-stopping true tale of an innocence stolen and a family torn apart – told by a woman who has finally managed to confront her harrowing past.

Someone she knew
Someone she trusted
Someone who betrayed her

The devastating true story of a shattered childhood

NON-FICTION / MEMOIR 978 0 7553 1799 8

DADDY'S LITTLE GIRL

JULIA LATCHEM-SMITH

Julia's family was a picture of respectability. To the
outside world it was middle class, decent, loving.
But her mother didn't love her enough. And her
father loved her too much.

Between the ages of eight and thirteen, Julia's father
sexually abused her. Loyal to her family, and desperate to
keep it intact, the abuse had to become their little secret.
Even as Julia struggled to come to terms with her ordeal, she
knew that revealing the truth would rip her family apart.

When she finally cried out for help, she was encouraged
to retract her allegations and branded a liar. In her
teenage years, she began to doubt her own sanity.
Had the abuse really happened? Her father couldn't
have done that . . . could he?

This is the harrowing story of how Julia's father abused
her trust, and cheated her of her childhood. But it is
also the uplifting story of how, years later, Julia
successfully confronted her painful past and began
to carve out for herself a meaningful future.

NON-FICTION / MEMOIR 978 0 7553 1638 0

More Non-fiction from Headline Review

FOR THE LOVE OF MY MOTHER

J. P. RODGERS

A truly gripping tale told by the son she thought she'd lost forever, *For The Love of My Mother* is a story of triumphing over poverty, of hope when there seems to be none, and a tribute to a mother's love for her son.

Bridie Rodgers was just two years old when she was arrested for begging on the streets of Dublin – she was to spend the next thirty years of her life locked away in institutions.

The orphanage came first, then after being raped and falling pregnant she was sent to a home for unmarried mothers. After giving birth to a son, John, Bridie's child was taken away from her, and she was sent to one of Ireland's infamous Magdalene Laundries. This was only the beginning . . .

They took her freedom.

They took her innocence.

They took her child.

But they couldn't take her spirit.

NON-FICTION / MEMOIR 978 0 7553 1593 2